BEST OF BRITISH

Maurice Sellar, Lou Jones,
Robert Sidaway and Ashley Sidaway

Stills researched by Carrie Haines
With a foreword by Barry Brown

SPHERE BOOKS LIMITED

Sphere Books Limited, 27 Wrights Lane, London W8 5TZ

First published by Sphere Books Ltd 1987
Copyright © 1987 by Maurice Sellar, Lou Jones, Robert Sidaway
and Ashley Sidaway

TRADE
MARK

Designed and typeset in Joanna by
The Pen and Ink Book Co. Ltd, London
Printed and bound in Great Britain by
Hazell, Watson and Viney, Aylesbury

Contents

For Daniel,
who one day may share
our delightful world of fantasy

Foreword

In post-war Australia, as a teenager brought up on Hollywood movies of the 1930s and 1940s, I suddenly became aware of another kind of film with stories and characters I could relate to more easily. They seemed more real to me. What's more, most of the actors and actresses spoke beautifully. I began remembering their names – Margaret Lockwood, James Mason, Phyllis Calvert, John Mills, Jean Simmons – and titles – *In Which We Serve*, *Great Expectations*, *The Chiltern Hundreds*, *So Long at the Fair*.

These films, I noticed, were introduced by a muscular man brandishing in slow motion a hammer which he swung on to a gigantic gong before the words appeared 'J. ARTHUR RANK PRESENTS'.

Only years later, when I came to Britain, did I appreciate Rank's enormous contribution to British Cinema. How did the devout, teetotal Methodist son from a famous Yorkshire flourmilling family – a rather dour, conservative man, by all accounts – become a major influence on the films millions of people all round the world saw each week in their local cinema? Apparently it all started because he wanted to film John Bunyan's religious epic *The Pilgrim's Progress* – something he never achieved!

Consequently I was delighted when two independent producers, Robert Sidaway and Maurice Sellar, came to me at the BBC with a project called *Best of British* – ten programmes compiled from treasures in the now expanded J. Arthur Rank film library.

We agreed a thematic approach was best, and in the ensuing months the production team derived great pleasure from screening again all those movies which had so enthralled me in Australia all those years ago. They have made a delightful television series – and the show's writers and producers, who have also written the book, have expanded this to provide additional background information and interesting anecdotes to complement the wonderful array of photographs from what are often regarded as the golden years of British film-making.

Barry Brown
Head of Purchased Programmes,
BBC Television

David Niven in *Matter of Life and Death*, 1946

I

The Heroes

From Tom Brown to Bulldog Drummond, from Biggles to Bond, the British hero has been represented as schoolboy, sleuth, soldier, sailor, sky-pilot and spy. And the silver screen has paid a handsome tribute to them all. But the actors who played all these heroic figures also came in assorted shapes and sizes themselves. There was the romantic variety – tall, short, dark or fair, but always handsome, as epitomized by the likes of Stewart Granger, Anthony Steele, Michael Redgrave and Dirk Bogarde, who set the female filmgoers' hearts a-flutter. There were the men's men – tough and gritty, like Jack Hawkins, John Gregson and Peter Finch. And there were those who didn't fit into either of these two categories, but who, nevertheless, could play heroic roles with utter conviction, spicing up their parts with charm, like Leslie Howard and Robert Donat, with gutsiness like John Mills and Richard Attenborough, or with tongue-in-cheek humour like David Niven and Kenneth More. Throughout the late 1930s , the 1940s, 1950s and early 1960s, these men reigned supreme, and were Britain's top box-office stars. Yet their introductions into the film industry were as widely divergent as the roles they played. And, as we shall see, the heroic roles they portrayed on film were no match for the heroism many of them demonstrated in their offscreen lives.

Stewart Granger's real name was James Stewart, but he had to change it because another actor, whose real name was also James Stewart, was already a big star in Hollywood when Stewart Granger, as he now called himself, began to make a career in British films. He was born in the Old Brompton Road, London, on 6 May, 1913, the son of a Scottish Army officer. His mother had been a famous beauty and the daughter of actress Jane Emmerson, who had been a member of the legendary actor Henry Irving's company.

Granger originally had ambitions to become a doctor, but his family, living on his father's small pension, could not afford to send him through medical school. So he joined a repertory company as a juvenile lead, and went on to distinguish himself as a leading man in the highly respected Birmingham Repertory Company. He began in films as an extra, and coincidentally started on the same day as another actor who was to remain his 'best pal' to the end of his days, Michael Wilding. Both had taken up this somewhat odd occupation for the same reason: 'because you got a guinea a day, and the best crumpet in the world!'

Granger admitted that he had no ambition to become a serious film actor, let alone a star. He was in the business just for the fun. After making two uneventful films, he was cast in a costume drama that would establish him as one of the great romantic leads of

Stewart Granger in Caravan, 1946

1

John Gregson in *Sea of Sand*, 1958

Roger Livesey and Anton Walbrook in
The Life and Death of Colonel Blimp,
1943

Anthony Steele in *The Black Tent*, 1956

wartime, and of the immediate post-war British cinema. It was a film made by the Gainsborough Studios, called *The Man in Grey* (see chapter 6). It was originally intended that Robert Donat should play the part that Granger was to seize with both grateful hands, but Donat was busy on another picture, and it was he who recommended Granger to the director, Leslie Arliss. In one scene, Granger had to slap Margaret Lockwood across the face. He had to do this several times, as he just couldn't bring himself to hit her hard enough. Margaret kept encouraging him, and eventually he forgot his good breeding and the fact that he had been an officer in the Gordon Highlanders, as well as a very useful amateur boxer, and he gave her a resounding slap. It nearly knocked her cold but nursing her swollen jaw, Margaret gave him a weak 'thumbs up' sign, and the director gleefully shouted 'Print it'. It was that scene, more than anything else in the film, that the women cinema-goers loved, and it made Granger an overnight star. He was quickly placed under contract to Rank, and made several highly successful films with them – films such as *Love Story*, *Fanny by Gaslight*, *Madonna of the Seven Moons*, *Caravan* and *Waterloo Road*. In these last two, Granger was again asked to make use of his prowess in the ring for fight sequences. In all the fights and stunts he did, he rarely used a stuntman or double, preferring in the cause of realism to take the knocks, falls and bruises himself. He gives a splendidly skilful display of his pugilistic ability in *Caravan*, but has less success in *Waterloo Road*, where he plays the part of a wartime spiv who is dallying with soldier John Mills's wife. Mills goes absent without leave with the sole intention of giving Granger a thrashing. To this day their confrontation remains one of the most plausible fist-fights ever screened. It was co-ordinated by Dave Crowley, who was the ex-lightweight champion of Great Britain, and the sequence was rehearsed with Granger and Mills – also a very handy boxer – for a week before it was shot. For a rare change, Granger had to lose the fight, but privately he admitted that he absolutely hated the thought of losing, even though it was cinema make-believe.

Dirk Bogarde in *Tale of Two Cities*, 1958

Douglas Montgomery in *The Way to the Stars*, 1945

Dirk Bogarde and Marie Versini in *Tale of Two Cities*, 1958

Stewart Granger in *Woman Hater*, 1949

A few years later, when his star status took him to the Mecca of the film business, Hollywood, Granger had a real-life, and much more 'sinister', fight, which could easily have destroyed his career. He was at that time married to the beautiful actress, Jean Simmons, and she too had decided that Hollywood was the city where she could attain international celebrity. Howard Hughes, one of the richest men on earth, and certainly the most powerful in Hollywood, had secretly bought up Jean Simmons' contract from Rank, and was now pressurizing her to sign another long-term contract with him. Both Simmons and her husband were adamantly opposed to the idea, believing that long-term contracts did much more harm than good by limiting an actor's choice of roles.

Hughes used all his mighty legal muscle to prove that Jean Simmons had already got a 'moral' contract with him. But Granger, acting on her behalf, and against all the advice of everyone in 'Tinsel Town', who told him he would never work in the industry again, took Hughes to court. It created worldwide interest in the press – in one outburst in the witness box, Granger exploded that Hughes's case had nothing to do with 'moral contracts' or the studio he owned – it was purely that the mega-rich Hughes wanted to 'screw my wife'! Granger was naturally ticked off by the judge for using this kind of emotive language, but in toned-down version it captured all the headlines, and amazingly Hughes chickened out of appearing in the court, and withdrew his claim. Against overwhelming odds, Granger had won. It was a true-life scenario with more heroic qualities than any he had played on the silver screen.

below left, John Mills in *The Way to the Stars*, 1945

below, John Mills in *Waterloo Road*, 1944

John Mills was born at Watts Naval Training School for Boys on 22 February, 1908. He was, therefore, well schooled in naval procedure, spending his early years in that environment, and it probably accounts for the fact that he played so many roles about the Senior Service with such conviction. His first part ever in a film was that of a singing, dancing sailor called Midshipman Golightly in the film *Midshipmaid*. He played the part with such authority, having trained for many years in the theatre, that it took him on to a career in front of the camera which spanned more than eighty feature films – and in most of them he was the star. But it could all have been so different if he had not displayed enormous courage as a junior schoolboy boarder. For the chirpy confidence that characterizes so many of his later roles in film and theatre was literally being beaten out of him.

The son of a headmaster, Lewis Mills (John's real name) was sent to board at Norwich High School for Boys, after his father had taken a post at a school which he considered unsuitable as a place of learning for his own family. It was at Norwich that Mills was to meet the scourge of so many public schools at that time – the school bully. Mills was small in height and fair of face, which made him the perfect victim for the torment he was to endure for so long. Each night in the dorm, after 'lights out', this young sadist would inflict the most painful punishment on Mills, making him stand naked in the middle of the dorm holding a jug of cold water on his head, and beating him on the vulnerable parts of his anatomy should he just fractionally lower his arms. As so many children locked into this kind of nightmare find, it was considered cowardly to 'snitch' to the masters, and risk the contempt of other classmates. So Mills decided that his only course of action was to try to deal with the matter himself. His sister, Annette, ran a dancing academy at that time, and one of her dancing partners had been a daring First World War pilot. It was to him, whilst on a brief school holiday, that Mills turned, and blurted out his frightful experiences. The ex-pilot was an expert on ju-jitsu, so Mills couldn't have chosen a better champion for his sad cause.

Over a period of several days, the pilot gave Mills a crash course in the martial art, and by the time he returned to the school he was to some degree competent at it. On the night of his return the dreaded moment came when 'lights out' was called. The bully began his usual jeering and tormenting, telling Mills to strip off and go through his hour of agony. But this time Mills refused, and the eventful confrontation came about. It staggered everyone in the dorm – including the diminutive Mills, who, although still shaking like a leaf, set about the 'thug', using the much bigger boy's superior weight and height to hurl him around the room. Eventually Mills leaped on the dazed bully, locked him in an armhold, and nearly succeeded in banging his head through the floorboards.

The bully's face looked like a squashed tomato when a housemaster at last came into the dorm to break up the fight. There followed a full enquiry, and the bully was expelled. Mills was of course, reprimanded by the headmaster for brawling, but he also conceded that Mills had shown a good deal of pluck. He was, thereafter, a school hero in the true Tom Brown tradition.

Following in the footsteps of so many other major British film stars, Mills was placed under contract with the Rank Organization, and had enormous success with them, achieving international status in such films as *In Which We Serve*, *Great Expectations*, *This Happy Breed*, *The Way to the Stars*, and many, many others. It is ironic, perhaps, that it was not as the gutsy little hero, the role played to perfection in countless British films, that he won his coveted first Oscar, but for the performance he gave as the village idiot in David Lean's big panoramic motion picture *Ryan's Daughter* (1969). It must have been almost more of a challenge for him to play roles that did not require him to keep his upper and lower lip stiff as a brush, and he clearly relished these opportunities, rare though they were, when they came. As in the 1941 Anthony Asquith production *Cottage to Let*, where he plays a Nazi spy and, in a battle of wits, is unmasked by a Cockney evacuee (played by a youngster who also went on to distinguish himself as one of Britain's leading character actors, George Cole).

Now in his seventies, Mills is almost as active as ever, playing demanding roles in the theatre and on television, and leading character parts in films. From his early childhood, when he had to prove to himself that the disadvantages of being small in height did not mean that he was also small in terms of guts, John Mills has continued to shine as one of Britian's best loved and most admired stars. This was confirmed when the ultimate accolade which a British actor can receive was bestowed on him, and on 28 July 1976, Mr John Mills became Sir John Mills.

Another one of our great intrepid on- and off-screen British heroes, Kenneth More, entered the entertainment industry in a most unusual and, by his own admission, most enjoyable way. He began his illustrious career at the famed Windmill Theatre, London – the nursery of so many of our great British comedians. For Peter Sellers, Tony Hancock, Michael Bentine and a star-studded cast, all of whom cut their comedy teeth there, it was a rather painful business, for the Windmill customers really came to see the nubile, if immobile, nudes, and a comic had to be both original and very amusing to make 'em smile, never mind laugh. This was a problem that at first did not present itself to the young ex-apprentice engineer, Kenneth More, son of an RFC officer. He just had a great time moving all the scenery and watching all the gorgeous girls go by.

More was born on 20 September, 1914, when the First World War was about six weeks old. His father was a comparatively wealthy man, having inherited a fortune from his own father, but was good-hearted and over generous, and blew not one fortune, but also another which he inherited, this time from a maiden aunt.

However, in his early days, young More, his sister and mother lived in splendid style, with a cook, a nanny, chauffeur, butler and gardener, in a large house in Gerrards Cross. Before his father's circumstances changed dramatically for the worse, More had the

Director and producer of *A Night to Remember* (1958), Roy Baker and William MacQuitty

Kenneth More in *A Night to Remember*, 1958

6

benefit of a good education, but he clearly enjoyed sport more than his studies, and failed to attain any qualifications by the time he left school. But he had the grit, determination and, as some would say, obstinacy of one of his most distinguished ancestors, Sir Thomas More. Kenneth More was also friendly with the Queen, who, after an evening wining and dining at the Astors' country estate, in an uncharacteristic gesture kicked off her shoes, to prove to him that in spite of all the walking and standing she did on ceremonial occasions, she still had no bunions. More, unlike his ancestor, cherished his friendship with his monarch, and it is well known that she admired his ability as an actor, having attended many a film première in which he appeared.

He had come a long way from the Windmill Theatre where, after shifting scenery, and later acting as a 'feed' to some of the comedians, he had gone into provincial rep. From there he slowly graduated to more orthodox repertory companies, becoming more professional and polished as the years passed. His acting career was interrupted when he was called up into the Royal Navy, where he soon became a junior officer, and saw the kind of action which he later depicted in war films with such realism. He'd had, since he was a small boy, a recurring dream. It was one where he stood on the deck of a ship which was being dive-bombed by enemy planes. In this dream, or perhaps nightmare would be a more appropriate word, one of the planes dropped a bomb directly over him. As it was about to hit him, he woke up sweating profusely. Whilst he was standing on the ship *Aurora*, he experienced in real life the exact details of his dream, when the

ship was under attack from German Stukas, as they patrolled the Mediterranean. As the big bomb whistled its descent, More saw a Paramount newsreel cameraman filming the action close to his side. He immediately rugger-tackled the surprised man, and hurled him into a corner which he, too, dived into.

The bomb hit and exploded in the precise spot where the cameraman had been standing. More's dream had saved both their lives, and after this dramatic event the dream never occurred again. He was to portray this kind of believable heroism in so many of his film roles, and this was especially noticeable when he was playing the part of a real-life hero such as Douglas Bader, DSO, DFC, the great Second World War fighter ace, in the film *Reach for the Sky* (1956), or when he played the courageous second officer in *A Night to Remember* (1958) – the story of the sinking of the *Titanic*, when out of 2,208 passengers and crew, only 705 survived. Or as Lieutenant Evans in *Scott of the Antarctic* (1948), the film of the tragic expedition to the South Pole.

Kenneth More's last courageous battle, his own personal fight against a crippling disease, was the one which sadly he lost. But he will always be remembered with great affection by cinema audiences, and by those who knew him – for his extrovert personality, his natural wit and, above all, his endearing warmth.

Those same qualities could also be applied in different measures to David Niven. But, unlike so many who made the trip to the city of stars before and after him, Niven had no professional acting experience whatsoever, and plunged into Hollywood at the deep end. He signed on at the Central Casting Agency, and was listed as 'English type 2,008'. But the other 2,007 were tough competitors, and when at last he got a chance to take a screen test and was offered a contract, the Immigration Department stepped in, and Niven beat a hasty retreat on a Mexican-bound fruit train.

Kenneth More in *Northwest Frontier*, 1959

Kenneth More in *Reach for the Sky*, 1956

David Niven in *The Way Ahead*, 1949

David Niven was always a resourceful and determined man, qualities that admirably equipped him for the many heroic parts he played on the screen. His father was Scottish, his mother French, and he was born on 1 March, 1910. After spending most of his childhood in Scotland, he went to Stowe public school, and then to Sandhurst, with the intention of pursuing a military career. He sampled this as a young officer in the Highland Light Infantry, but after serving two years in an outpost in Malta became excruciatingly bored with the life of a peacetime soldier. So he left the Army, and began his search for real adventure by going to Canada. Thereafter he embarked on a series of different jobs. He worked on a newspaper, helped in bridge construction, was a waiter, a barman, and then, thinking this latter occupation gave him the necessary know-how, became a wine salesman and took off over the Canadian border to the USA. Again he became disenchanted with the wine and liquor business, and branched out in a new direction. This time he was offered a partnership in an indoor racing track in Atlantic City, but he was soon put out of business by the local Mafia, who made such big demands for protection that it was wiser to shut up shop.

Thinking himself lucky to get out in one piece, the restless Niven took off yet again in search of fresh fields. He followed the sun, and spent most of his time beachcombing in Bermuda and Havana, finding some extra excitement by becoming involved in a Peruvian revolution, fighting at various times for both sides. When the British Consul heard about his activities, he gave Niven twenty minutes to pack his bag and get out of the country. After this it took him four months of nomadic wandering before he could get back to America. When he finally did, he headed straight for Hollywood again, and an older and wiser English type 2,008 was once again prepared to join the queue looking for work.

At last he got a break. Sam Goldwyn saw him and put him under contract. A series of minor parts followed, consisting of such jewels as 'Hello my dear' in one film, and 'Goodbye, my dear' in another. But along came *Dodsworth*, and a part he could really get his very white teeth into. It launched him on a career which made him a household name. In 1939, when Britain declared war on Germany, Niven decided to put his Army training to patriotic use, and joined the British forces. Whilst actively serving his country, he only agreed to make two films, and this was because of their powerful propaganda message – *The First of the Few*, and *The Way Ahead* (see chapter 7).

David Niven and Kim Hunter in *A Matter of Life and Death*, 1946

In 1946 Niven made his first film for that formidable duo, Michael Powell and Emeric Pressburger, *A Matter of Life and Death*. It was a film that created many precedents for the British cinema. It tells the story of Squadron Leader Peter D. Carter (David Niven) who is the last surviving crew member of a crippled Lancaster bomber. Realizing he can no longer remain with his aircraft, he contacts base to reveal his position and hopeless plight, and engages in a touching, and often deeply moving, two-way radio conversation with the WAAF wireless operator. (The twenty-three year old Kim Hunter, who played the WAAF, was the first American actress to appear in a British film since before the War, and had been tested by Powell and Pressburger when they were in the States getting background material for the film.) Niven, as the crashed pilot, is rushed into an operating theatre, and whilst his life hovers in the balance we are taken into his mind as it drifts into a world of fantasy, culminating in a vast courtroom trial to decide whether he should live or die. The most imaginative and expensive sets were created to depict the 'other world', including a giant staircase of 106 steps, each one twenty feet wide. It operated like an elevator and was driven by a 12 h.p. engine. The huge apparatus, which was totally functional, had been constructed by a famous firm of engineers, and the whole process was kept a closely guarded secret by the cast and crew, and given the code name 'Operation Ethel'.

A Matter of Life and Death was the first Royal Command film, and its première in Leicester Square caused such a crush, with thousands turning up to see the stars, and catch a glimpse of the King and Queen, that the police, who were totally unprepared for such numbers, almost lost control, and the Royal family had to be rushed through into the foyer in most unregal fashion, nearly being

A Matter of Life and Death, 1946

trampled under foot in the process. The King was badly shaken by the experience, as indeed were some of the stars, whose clothes and stockings had been torn to shreds by the excited crowds.

Niven returned to Hollywood and resumed his career there. It continued to flourish, and he made many box office hits. In 1959, with Deborah Kerr as his co-star in *Separate Tables*, Niven won an Academy Award and the New York Critics' Award for his outstanding performance. Later on in life, this natural, witty raconteur turned his talent to writing, and his autobiography became an international best seller. Niven brought all the finest attributes of the British hero to the roles that he played; he had dash and charm, liberally laced with a puckish sense of fun, and by all accounts, that was his off-screen personality as well.

To many filmgoers, the archetypal British hero was personified by Jack Hawkins. But he began his professional career as a child actor in roles which were almost the antithesis of those in which he later became famous. He was signed up by Madame Italia Conti and, in addition to playing pageboy-type parts, he took ballet and singing classes. It was, in fact, as a pageboy in George Bernard Shaw's *St Joan* that he got his first West End theatre break, having been auditioned for it by the great playwright himself.

Hawkins was born on 14 September, 1910 at a terraced house in Lyndhurst Road, Wood Green, London, the son of a master builder. He learned his considerable acting craft after many years in the theatre, and under the strict, but always kindly, guidance of the actor-managers Sybil Thorndike and Lewis Casson, acknowledged at that time as the best husband-and-wife theatre team in the world. It was in the part of St George in *Where the Rainbow Ends* that Hawkins played his first stage hero, and it gave him the taste for playing this type of man – one with sterling chivalry and leadership qualities. In time, he developed this character with such a fine art that when he had the opportunities to play heroic roles in films, it was as though they had been specially written for him – they fitted him like a Savile Row suit of armour!

Irony seems to have played more than an unusually large part in Hawkins's personal life. Although his name immediately conjures up vivid mental pictures of Hawkins, the rugged sea skipper; Hawkins, the straightbacked Army colonel; Hawkins, the hawk-eyed RAF Group Captain – in fact, to quote Hawkins himself, 'I played enough senior officers to stock the whole Ministry of Defence' – in real life he had the devil's own job to enlist in the services. He was at first, it seems, rejected by all the fighting forces, having volunteered after watching thousands of troops returning from the evacuation of Dunkirk. At last he was accepted by the Royal Welsh Fusiliers, and though he may have looked every inch an officer, it was as a lowly private that Hawkins was enrolled. Not having attended any of the acceptable public schools, nor even RADA, he found it was some time before his obvious officer potential was noted, but by the end of the War he had worked his way up to full colonel.

After the War, Hawkins went back to the theatre, and during one

Jack Hawkins in *The Malta Story*, 1953

of his performances Alexander Korda saw him, and signed him to a three-year contract. Slowly, through a series of costume dramas, he began to establish himself. But it was in the part of Ericson, the Commander of a corvette in the film *The Cruel Sea* (1952) that he became a film star of international status. At about this time, he was signed to the Rank Organization, and thus began the roles with which the filmgoing public will always associate him. No one ever played a British officer better than Hawkins; no actor ever brought such authority to these roles. In 1954 he was voted the No. 1 British box-office name. And much to his amusement, a critic wrote: 'Hawkins makes love better to a battleship than to a woman.'

It was as a founder director of Allied Film Makers, along with Brian Forbes and Richard Attenborough, that Hawkins was able to combine all his knowledge and talent for playing service officers, in the role of an embittered ex-Army Major, who collects a group of former wartime veterans around him with the sole intention of carrying out an audacious bank raid. The *League of Gentlemen* (1960–61) was based on a novel by John Holland, adapted for the screen by Brian Forbes, directed by Basil Deardon and produced by Michael Relph. It was an instant success and well justified Rank's high production cost of £1 million in terms of box-office receipts. However, it took a toll on Hawkins's health that could never be equated, for it was during the making of this picture that Hawkins began to have trouble with his throat. The condition was particularly aggravated during the filming of the bank raid sequence, which took three days to shoot, mostly in dense smoke.

Jack Hawkins in *The League of Gentlemen*, 1960

When Hawkins finally went to a specialist, his condition was diagnosed as cancer of the throat. He had a choice: either an immediate operation in which he would have to have his larynx removed, or certain death within a short space of time. This, of course, was a terrible dilemma for Hawkins, which can be likened to a concert pianist losing his hands, or a great painter suddenly blinded. But Hawkins's courage was not just for the screen. He went through with the operation and, with the same determination his characters always demonstrated, he won this first round for survival. Without any means of vocal communication, Hawkins began to fret, and when the chance came to have an electronic voicebox inserted in his throat, although there was only a fifty-fifty chance that he would pull through the operation, he did not hesitate. However, this time the odds were not good enough, and in the summer of 1973 the legendary film warrior fought and lost his battle against the last enemy.

There can be little doubt that the most celebrated of all British heroes was Leslie Howard. Although always regarded as the quintessential Englishman, in reality Howard was of Hungarian extraction, his father, Frank Stainer, having emigrated to Britain in the late 1880s. Howard was often amused by his ultra-English image, which was also his off-screen persona. But he never tried to conceal his Hungarian ancestry, and in fact was very proud of it, believing that it contributed to the artistic side of his nature. His father, who was a clerk in the City, used to supplement his meagre income by giving piano lessons to well-brought-up young ladies. One of these young ladies, Lilian, eventually became Mrs Frank Stainer, Leslie's mother, and Leslie made his début in the world in London on 3 April, 1893.

Although a very shy boy who was compelled to wear glasses at a very early age, being exceedingly shortsighted (an advantage to film actors, especially in camera close-ups), young Leslie loved to write shows and entertain his parents, relatives and friends in concerts which he would present in the garden of the family home. But much as he enjoyed the applause and the laughter from these amateur ventures, he never wanted to take up acting as a profession. Indeed, throughout his lifetime he expressed an absolute hatred of acting, believing it to be an 'embarrassing occupation' and 'women's work'. He had always cherished a dream of becoming a successful writer, and was constantly to be found scribbling in his notebook. When he left Dulwich College at the age of nineteen, he explained to his father that he would like to contemplate a career as a writer. But his father would not even discuss it, telling him to seek a respectable position, and so Leslie started earning his first crust working as a lowly clerk in Cox's Bank. He loathed every minute of it. When, in 1914, Britain went to war with Germany, Howard, like so many young men, could not wait to volunteer, and as he didn't fancy endless drilling and marching he volunteered for the Cavalry. The fact that he had only ever ridden a seaside donkey in his life before did not deter him. He would do anything to get away from that bank.

In the event, after taking a good number of bumps and falls, Leslie became a first-class horseman, and ended up as a Second Lieutenant. But he did not have a 'good' war. He was thrown into the thick of it in France, and saw many of his comrades lose their lives in the endless massacres of attack and counter-attack. He himself was invalided back to England after suffering from 'severe shell shock'. Whilst convalescing, he took up writing again, and later he submitted his writings to various publishers – and got the inevitable rejections. But he was determined never to go back to the bank, or take on similarly mundane work, and remembering his amateur dramatic days, he decided he would have a go at becoming a professional actor. Amazingly, the first theatrical agent's door on which he knocked, produced a part for him. It was in a fifth-rate touring production of *Peg o' My Heart*. Leslie jumped at the chance and at the £4.4s.0d. a week he would get. It was then he decided to change his name from Stainer to Howard, and although this production did not affirm that a star was born, it could be said that his appealing laid-back style was created in embryo during the endless weeks of the tour, where they performed to half-empty seaside resorts, and to half-full theatres in industrial towns.

It is true to say that Howard saw the enormous potential of the 'kinema' at a very early period in the emerging film industry. So much so that he persuaded the great English character actor, C. Aubrey Smith, and the famous writer A.A. Milne, along with the up-and-coming director Adrian Brunel, to form a film company that would rival the American moguls. Howard would be at the helm, and they called themselves Minerva Films Ltd. Under this banner several little one-act dramas were produced, and although they didn't exactly shake the universe, the experience did arouse in Leslie Howard a passionate interest in the new art form that he was

Leslie Howard in *49th Parallel*, 1941

never to lose. Not before many years, though, did Howard become what would now be termed a 'cinema superstar'.

He went to Hollywood in the early 1930s , and made a series of entirely forgettable films. Wishing to forget the experience himself, he returned to England, where he made even more forgettable films. But all the time he was learning his craft, polishing his performances, and becoming increasingly fascinated by film writing and directing. He had, however, become a big name on the London stage, indeed a matinée idol, and it was only the superb script of Somerset Maugham's classic, *Of Human Bondage*, that tempted him back to the 'City of the Angels', as he persisted in calling Los Angeles. He was very disappointed at first with the casting of the female lead. She was supposed to be Cockney, and here they had this unknown American actress. He is on record as saying, 'It was ridiculous casting – shocking.' After acting just one big scene with her, he changed his mind. The girl was brilliant, and with his usual unassuming charm he admitted happily that she would steal the picture. She very nearly did. Her name was Bette Davis. The film also launched, in the true Hollywood tradition, Leslie Howard.

From this moment on, Leslie Howard was box-office, and other big hits followed in rapid succession. *The Scarlet Pimpernel*, Baroness Orczy's outwardly fey, inwardly tough-as-old-boots English hero of the French revolution, Sir Percy Blakeney, and then on to *The Petrified Forest*, where he played a resilient character that, as he said, 'could have been written just for me'. But it is clearly for his performance as Ashley in (arguably) the most successful motion picture of all time, *Gone with the Wind*, that he established himself as one of Hollywood's immortals. When the Second World War broke out the year after the release of this epic, Howard and his entire family moved back to England. He wanted to be part of the fight for freedom. Too old to be called up, he felt he might be of assistance in trying to counteract Goebbels's barrage of propaganda, and in particular his radio puppet, William Joyce, known in Britain as 'Lord Haw-Haw'.

Leslie Howard and Eric Portman in *49th Parallel*, 1941

Howard began a weekly series of broadcasts for the BBC called 'Britain Speaks'. In these, he addressed himself to the North American continent, urging listeners to help in the Allies' fight against the tyranny of Nazism. His beautiful, well-modulated voice was perfect for radio, and the talks achieved a great following. Winston Churchill was most impressed, and so, it seems, was Adolf Hitler, who had Howard immediately placed on his death list. But the broadcasts were not enough for Howard: he wanted to do more for the cause. In the event, he made four more films, all supported by the MOI and aimed at achieving the maximum propaganda value. Among these were *The 49th Parallel* and *The Gentle Sex* (see chapter 7).

In the spring of 1943, Anthony Eden, the Foreign Secretary, asked Howard if he would go to Portugal and Spain and give a series of lectures. It was vital to Britain that these two countries should remain neutral in the war. It was felt that Howard, by talking about his career, would be able to expound the virtues of democracy. Whilst loath to leave his family, he felt it was his duty to go, though it was always made clear to him that there was a risk; the Luftwaffe constantly attacked civilian aircraft at this time. Howard landed safely enough, the lectures were well received, and he was looking forward to returning to his beloved England. That he never did, is now part of filmland folklore. On the flight out of Lisbon to London in June 1943, somewhere over the Bay of Biscay, the commercial airliner Howard was on, which had a full passenger load including two small children, was attacked by a formation of eight Luftwaffe fighters. There was not so much as a pea-shooter on board the passenger plane to retaliate with, and it was blown to pieces in the sky.

There has been a lot of mystery surrounding this attack, with the main question always being – why should eight German planes have gone so far out of their way to bring down just one civilian aircraft? One rumour has it that the Germans had received information that Churchill was on board the plane, another that Howard had really been on a spying mission and was bringing back vital information.

The mystery has never been solved to this day. Whatever the reason, Howard gave his life for Britain. He knew the risk involved, and it did not deter him from doing what he felt was his duty. On-screen he was a romantic figure, strong in a gentle way. He imbued his roles with an intelligent firmness, and could achieve more through his shyly reassuring manner than many a Hollywood tough guy, twice his weight and build, could manage with his fists. Although when cornered he would never avoid a physical confrontation, he showed us all how brain could overcome brawn. C.A. Lejeune, the film critic, wrote this about him: 'Probably no single war casualty has induced in the public of these islands such an acute sense of personal loss. Howard was more than just a popular actor. Since the war he has become something of a symbol to the British people.' An epitaph that this true patriot would have been proud of, even if vaguely amused by it.

2

The All-singing, All-dancing Show

For too many years it used to be considered that when it came to the stage and screen musical, the Americans had no equal, and this was regrettably all too true. But it certainly wasn't always so, and happily nowadays it is no longer so again. It cannot be denied that Britain went through a rather bad patch in this highly specialized field of entertainment. That this country has re-emerged, if anything more triumphant than ever, can be confirmed by a casual glance through any national newspaper's West End theatre columns. Here there is positive proof that the London stage abounds with lively, tuneful, high-kicking shows – and most of these productions, which are world-class, are home-grown. This should come as no surprise to anyone other than the most devoted *aficionados* of the US musical, because the musical, as we know it today, was born here in Britain. Its roots are firmly planted in the tradition of seventeenth-century productions such as *The Beggar's Opera*.

But the musicals that we all know today owe more than anything to the works of those legendary Victorian establishment figures, William Gilbert and Arthur Sullivan. They were the first real words-and-music men in the modern sense. As such, their contribution to the twentieth-century musical is recognized in full by such great American popular music composers as Cole Porter, Frank Loesser, Richard Rodgers, Lorenz Hart and Oscar Hammerstein, all of whom have at some time or other in their brilliant careers acknowledged their debt to Messrs. Gilbert and Sullivan. It was only in the late 1930s that Britain began to develop a deep inferiority complex about our ability to match the Americans. We began to believe that our writers of popular songs were not good enough, that our dancers just didn't have 'that natural rhythm', and our choreographers were too schooled in the ways of classical ballet to invent eye-catching, daring and dashing dance routines. Fortunately, Britain produced screen musicals in the 1930s that often were as good, and sometimes a good deal better, than anything that came out of Hollywood. That undeniable proof is preserved on film and is happily undiminished by time.

One of the legends of British musicals is a star who shone so brightly that Hollywood constantly beckoned. She refused the call all her life, and because of that her sparkling talent was employed to

Jean Kent in *Trottie True*, 1949

18

Jessie Matthews in *Evergreen*, 1934

the full in some wonderful British film musicals. Her name was Jessie Matthews.

But this glittering gamine star, who became the darling of three continents, could not have started in show business in a more humble way. She was born in a tiny Soho flat, No. 94, Berwick Street, on Monday 11 March, 1907. She was one of ten surviving children out of a total of sixteen. Her running order at the time of her birth was number seven. Her father owned a greengrocery stall opposite their flat, in the famous Berwick Street Market, and Jessie, like all her family, had a strong Cockney accent. Later on this vanished entirely as Jessie became known, not only for her breathtaking dancing and her charming singing, but also for her precise, ultra-posh elocution. Her climb to fame – and it was fame that few female British musical stars have ever equalled; Gertrude Lawrence, Evelyn Laye, Anna Neagle and, much later, Julie Andrews, were probably the only contenders – began at a very slow pace.

Coming from such poverty gave Jessie a determination to succeed, but because of her background it was far from easy. She was, however, born with wonderful physical assets, an elfin beauty, large sparkling eyes and a body that appeared to be boneless. Jessie could make dancing seem entirely effortless. She could kick higher and more attractively than any dancer before or since. Only a Pavlova had her kind of natural ability in this exacting physical art. She began ballet dancing at the age of ten, and startled her teachers with her stunning gifts, performing exercises in her first lesson that it took most of her fellow pupils more than a year to achieve. She made her professional debut some two years later in a children's play called *Bluebell in Fairyland*, a Seymour Hicks production at the famous old music hall, the Metropolitan Theatre in Edgware Road, where she was following literally in the footsteps of Marie Lloyd, who had trodden those same boards only a few weeks earlier.

At the age of sixteen, Jessie was a 'standby chorus girl' in the

Jean Simmons in *The Way to the Stars*, 1945

Jessie Matthews in *Sailing Along*, 1938

show *London Calling*. Its star, Gertrude Lawrence, and the best high kickers in the line were chosen by the impresario André Charlot to open a new revue on Broadway. Jessie this time was promoted to full chorus lady. The revue was a smash hit, and established the careers of Gertrude Lawrence and Jack Buchanan in America. But Jessie herself had to wait patiently for almost five years for the vehicle that was to propel her to stardom. That opportunity came in the Noel Coward revue *This Year of Grace*, which opened in London at the Pavilion on 22 March, 1928. Her co-star was Sonny Hale, who was later to be her husband. But enormous scandal was created before that happy event, because at the time of their 'engagement', Sonny Hale was already married to another big musical star, Evelyn Laye. The divorce action captured worldwide headlines when the judge insisted that Jessie's love letters be read aloud in open court, and made cutting remarks about her character after hearing them.

Painful as this kind of exposure was to Jessie – she was to claim that 'the scars would remain with her for ever' – it did nothing to detract public interest from her talent, and after a series of small parts in films, she was taken under the wing of Victor Saville. It was Saville who saw the enormous movie potential of Jessie when he was looking for a girl to play Susie Dean in the film version of J.B. Priestley's *Good Companions*. Saville himself was without doubt Britain's leading musical film director, and at the time of his search was working for Gaumont British. In the company of producer Michael Balcon, often regarded as the British film industry's first 'tsar', he watched some of Jessie's rushes and knew that this girl was not only right for the part, but that she would be a major film box-office attraction. They were proved right, and one film success followed another with amazing regularity – films such as *Gangway*, *Head over Heels*, *It's Love Again*. In the film *Sailing Along* which, owing to the impending threat of the Second World War and her failing health, was her last screen musical for twenty years, there was a brilliantly staged routine choreographed by Buddy Bradley. It started with a tap dance, switched to mime, and then to ballet. Its 'on-screen time' was seven minutes, and Jessie and her American partner, Jack Whiting, danced for nearly a mile with the camera tracking them across a set so large that it had to be built over two vast sound stages. To this day, it is regarded as one of the finest dance routines ever to be captured on celluloid – on either side of the Atlantic.

But it was, perhaps, in the film *Evergreen*, based on her stage role, that she really reached her pinnacle. The film, which was directed by Victor Saville and choreographed by Buddy Bradley, with numbers such as 'Dancing on the Ceiling' by Richard Rodgers and Lorenz Hart, and 'Over My Shoulder' by Harold Woods – a song that was evermore to be associated solely with her – had them queueing at all prices. But it could have marked an even greater turning-point in her career, and one on which we can now only conjecture. For when Fred Astaire and his sister Adele, his dancing partner at the time, went to see Jessie in the show *One Damn Thing after Another*, Adele, who was thinking of getting married and

Jessie Matthews in *Evergreen*, 1934

retiring, said to Jessie, 'If I do leave, promise you'll take my place. You'll make a perfect partner for Fred!' When *Evergreen* was being planned, Victor Saville went to see Astaire to offer him the co-starring role with Jessie. Fred leaped at the idea, but RKO had signed him to a long-term contract and refused to release him. Had they done so, it would have been Fred Astaire and Jessie Matthews who danced those wonderful routines in *Evergreen*, instead of the very able, but far from spectacular, Barry Mackay. It is intriguing to imagine that, had Saville's idea of teaming Astaire and Matthews materialized, there would have been no need for Fred to hunt for a new partner (who, as it happened, turned out to be Ginger Rogers), and film fans the world over might have spoken in awe of the magic of Fred and Jessie. But that, as they say – and Jessie would have been the first wistfully to agree – is show business!

If Jessie was Britain's greatest song-and-dance lady of the 1930s, then one of her partners was unquestionably the most successful and internationally known British song-and-dance man of them all. His name was Jack Buchanan. He was born in the last century, in 1891, when Queen Victoria was still on the throne, yet he will always be associated with the sauve sophisticated style of the 1930s. He was to Britain what Maurice Chevalier was to France, and Fred Astaire to the United States. With his nasal way of singing, and long-legged effortless dancing, he soon became a favourite of the West End stage musical. In fact, he was dubbed 'Mr West End'. His debonair charm and good looks made him a natural for films, and it was not long before he was recruited into the industry and his talents fully exploited.

As a very young man Buchanan had acted in a couple of totally forgettable silent movies: *Auld Lang Syne* (1917), *Her Heritage* (1919), and so on. But it was with the advent of sound that he really came into his own. He was already a name on Broadway, having gone there with Beatrice Lillie and Gertrude Lawrence in an André Charlot and Archie Selwyn revue. But it was Jack who caught the Hollywood scout's eye, and he was soon in front of the camera doing what he did best, 'hoofing and singing', in the first of his many film musicals, *Show of Shows* (1929), and in the next year *Monte Carlo*. That was followed by the film for which he will probably always be remembered, mainly because of his hit recording of the title song, 'Goodnight Vienna'.

It was no secret in the gossipy world of show business that Buchanan and Jessie Matthews had no love for each other. This was due to the fact that Jessie always preferred her 'perfect' dancing partner and husband, Sonnie Hale, to Jack, and naturally enough, Jack resented it. Nevertheless, such was their drawing power to theatre audiences that, often against their wishes, they found themselves co-starring with each other. One such occasion did, however, have a happy outcome for an unknown dancer who sat demurely in the wings patiently waiting for her big break. It happened one evening, whilst the pair were entertaining in a supper-time cabaret, singing a popular song of the time, 'Fancy our Meeting', with love in their eyes as they gazed adoringly at each

right, Jessie Matthews in *Sailing Along*, 1938

far right, Jessie Matthews and Jack Whiting in *Sailing Along*, 1938

bottom right, Jessie Matthews in *Over My Shoulder*, 1934

Jean Kent in *Trottie True*, 1949

22

other, and, as Jessie said, 'with murder in our hearts'. Suddenly Jack recognized a friend at one of the tables and, right in the middle of their act, went gliding over to him and had a little chat. This was too much for Jessie, who stormed off, shouting that Jack could find someone else to partner him in future – or words to that effect. The girl who was in the wings, and whose name at the time was Marjorie Robertson, at last had her chance, and it was she who took over from Jessie as Jack's partner, and soon became a huge star herself – not of course as Marjorie Robertson, but under the name she changed to, Anna Neagle. Anna Neagle later became a Dame of the British Empire, and was loved and respected by all her fellow performers. But back to Jack. Such trifles as this he took in his long elegant stride. In fact, it is almost true to say that he rarely put a foot wrong, and in 1953, at the no-longer-tender age of sixty-two, he co-starred in his most successful film musical, *The Bandwagon*. The other star was Fred Astaire. It was directed by Liza's father, Vincent Minelli, and it was a smash hit on both sides of the Atlantic. No one could handle a top hat and cane better than Jack, with the possible exception of Fred himself, and here they were together, going through their smooth paces in some wonderful routines. The film will always be remembered for one of its big songs which has almost become the show business national anthem, 'That's Entertainment', the other one, perhaps, being Irving Berlin's 'There's no Business like Show Business'.

That same year, Jack returned to Britain and again starred in a colourful musical, *As Long as They're Happy*. Jack Buchanan's name will always be synonymous with style, and when 'old timers' in show business say, with a knowing smile, that they don't make entertainers like Jack any more, just one glance at some of his best musical movies will define exactly what they mean.

A young lady who also co-starred with Jack in *As Long as They're Happy* was sensible enough to change her real name before she did so. Somehow she assumed that Jean Shufflebottom would just not look good in lights. Jeannie Carson, on the other hand – the name she changed it to – did look exceedingly good in lights, and Jeannie, who made some popular films in Britain as a song-and-dance star, two of which were *An Alligator Named Daisy* (1956) and *Rockets Galore* (1957), took off to the USA. There she was an even bigger success, and starred on Broadway before going to Hollywood and playing in the title role of a top-rated television comedy series, *Hey, Jeannie*. This highly talented lady, noted for her effervescent personality, has so far not returned to these shores. Sad, really, because with Britain again in the forefront of stage musicals, her verve and her tuneful voice would surely be a major attraction.

George Robey could quite comfortably be placed in one of three categories – a fine character actor, the most highly rated music-hall comedian of his generation, or, as he appeared in the autumn of his life, a film star in British film musicals. On the halls, his top billing proudly proclaimed him to be the 'Prime Minister of Mirth', and for more than four decades he had audiences roaring with laughter at his risqué, *double entendre* jokes, a forerunner in style of Max

Margaret Lockwood in *I'll be your
Sweetheart*, 1945

George Robey in *Chu Chin Chow*, 1934

Miller, Frankie Howerd and Max Wall. Few have equalled his outrageous antics as a pantomine dame. Then suddenly this great clown switched from what was then termed 'low' comedy to classic drama, and many observers of his day believe no one has ever played Shakespeare's Falstaff better than Robey.

Robey's song at the end of his long act, 'If you were the only girl in the world', still rates among the evergreens of music-hall signature tunes. Only Marie Lloyd's 'Follow the Van' or Albert Chevalier's 'My Old Dutch' perhaps bear comparison. And it was his confident voicing of a sentimental love song that made him a natural choice, even though he was by then almost sixty-three years old, to star as Ali Baba in the screen version of the smash-hit British stage show *Chu Chin Chow*. The director was the former silent-screen comedian Walter Forde, and he and Robey got along like a house on fire, sharing an understanding of the art of comic timing. The film of *Chu Chin CHow* had an enormous international success with its spectacular effects and catchy melodies. So successful was it, in fact, and so splendid was Robey's performance, that the following year Sir Alexander Korda signed Robey to a three-year contract, proudly pronouncing, 'I regard George Robey as capable of rivalling in popularity any film star in the world. I have been considering for some time past the possibility of presenting him as a first rank film star.' It would be impossible today to imagine anyone being presented with this sort of opportunity of stardom in a new medium at the age of almost sixty-five. But then, of course, George Robey was very special, and this was affirmed when he became the first music-hall comedian to attain a knighthood.

Tessie O'Shea in *London Town*, 1947

Cicely Courtneidge in *Aunt Sally*, 1934

Much has been written about the formidable team of Michael Powell and Emeric Pressburger, those ex-patriot Hungarians who took the British cinema industry by its well-tailored collar and shook new life into it as writers, producers and directors – titles which they shared uniquely and jointly on all their major films for their Archers Production Company. Always highly innovative – using Powell's remarkable skill in producing stunning visual affects, such as those he provided in *The Thief of Bagdad* for Korda, and later in *A Matter of Life and Death* for his own company – the pair went into production with the first full-length story feature ballet film *The Red Shoes* (1948). Almost forty years on, the film still remains for most lovers of ballet the only one ever to capture the true essence of the world of dance, with its magical allure and total dedication to its form. It featured a dazzling new star, Moira Shearer, who already had enchanted audiences at the Royal Ballet, but who had never, before *The Red Shoes*, acted in front of a camera. With the impresario Lermantov played with power and conviction by Anton Walbrook, and Moira Shearer in the role of the ballet-crazed Vicky Page, the film established early on the almost fanatical zeal that is required by a budding prima ballerina, not only to get to the top, but, once she is there, to remain there.

'Why do you want to dance, Miss Page?' Lermantov asks her with barely concealed disdain.

'Why do you want to live, Mr Lermantov?' replies Vicky with all-consuming passion.

The designer was Heinz Heckroth, and the film was photographed in lovely pastel colours by Jack Cardiff. It also had an original score by Brian Easdale, which was conducted by the legendary Sir Thomas Beecham. The screenplay by Pressburger drew heavily on the true story of the *Ballet russe*, and in particular Diaghilev's traumatic relationships with some of his artists. The brilliant central ballet was created and choreographed by Robert Helpmann.

Whether they were lovers of ballet or merely average cinema-goers, *The Red Shoes* made audiences gasp with admiration. Its climactic scene again owes its origin to a true-life incident, for when Vicky Page dies on the night she is billed to make her triumphant comeback, a spotlight, not an understudy, takes over her role, poignantly showing us that this magical dancer was irreplaceable. This actually happened, when the greatest of all ballerinas, the incomparable Anna Pavlova, died on the night of a scheduled performance: her part, too, was played on that night by an ethereal white spotlight. *The Red Shoes* has reached cult status as a film, and it is not surprising that in the year of its release it was nominated for no less than four Oscars. No ballet film had ever won such acclaim before, or, for that matter, has done since.

Britain's contribution to the film musical can never be underestimated. The musical was at its strongest, perhaps, at a time when its audiences were very receptive, in the depressed 1930s, when 'escapism' was what they came to the cinema for, and the makers of British film musicals gave them just that, with dance routines full of sparkle and vitality, catchy songs and imaginative photography, and some stunning visual effects. And the public loved every minute of it, leaving the cinemas with a song in their hearts, and a spring in their heels, whistling their merry way home.

Kay Kendall in *London Town*, 1947

3

The English Roses

Margaret Lockwood in *The Wicked Lady*, 1945

Phyllis Calvert and Stewart Granger in *Madonna of the Seven Moons*, 1944

This rare and delicate flower finally perished in the early 1960s when sturdier strains from California, France and Italy took root on the cinema screen ... 'The English Rose' in film terms never existed. It has always been a well-coined media catch-phrase, thrown at Britain's most beautiful and talented leading actresses, and it has irritated and sometimes infuriated the 'roses' themselves.

In 1953 Deborah Kerr was quoted in a national newspaper: 'Film people concluded I wasn't a woman but a "lady", consequently anaemic, prissy, frigid and given to wearing Victorian unmentionables.' That same year she made *From Here To Eternity*, playing a turbulent adulteress, with the famous love-making on the beach scene with Burt Lancaster. But since that film, and although she has played a wide variety of characters on a broad emotional range and has been nominated for an Oscar six times, an English newspaper in 1963 still reported: 'Whether she likes it or not, and I suspect she doesn't, Deborah Kerr is still considered the sweetest English rose this country has ever exported.' And recently, whilst making the television programme *Deborah Kerr: Not Just an English Rose*, she confessed to still being irked by her English Rose image – 'I played nymphomaniacs as well as nuns you know.'

So did all Britain's female stars from the late 1930s to the late 1950s. Well, not all played nymphomaniacs, but they all played nuns at some point or other! And yes, they did have a very special beauty that shone when they were playing their 'girl next door' or 'innocent abroad' parts, and yet underlying all the work they did there was an undeniable 'I am in charge' quality which English audiences fully appreciated. So much so that during the 1940s the biggest star was undoubtedly Margaret Lockwood. The 'Wicked Lady' of the cinema was already a star through *The Man in Grey* and *Love Story* when she made *The Wicked Lady*, a film universally panned by the critics as 'salacious and bawdy', but which she simply described as 'a rollicking old romp' and through which, much more successfully than Deborah Kerr, she was able to throw off the 'English rose' tag. She even made certain that her beauty spot remained on her left cheek thereafter, reminding audiences that this actress with the flashing, liquid eyes controlled a passion that was anything but rose-like.

As with Phyllis Calvert, who in 1945 desperately wanted to play the 'split-personality' role of Rosanna/Madalena in *Madonna of the Seven Moons*. She so badly wanted to get away from one 'goody' part after another that she forced the studio photographer to portray her in both aspects of the part. She got it; and audiences were swayed away from the sweet, loving actress who, up until that moment, both on and off the screen, had behaved impeccably, and

Patricia Roc and Peter Murray-Hill in
Madonna of the Seven Moons, 1944

Phyllis Calvert and Stewart Granger in
Fanny by Gaslight, 1944

who had served the hype so efficiently by giving them an unquestionably perfect English rose. Her family and private life, out of choice, created an on-off film career, which meant, in her own words, that she was happy to 'play a couple of mums a year' and that she was reported 'not to have deserted the garden...she goes straight out to water the beans, cut and pack lettuces on returning from the studio'. She may have been irritated by being called a rose, but she certainly didn't help her own class.

Nor did Patricia Roc, though in her case there was absolutely nothing at all she could do about it. Although you could detect at times, the 'I am in charge' quality when she was playing 'being brave in love' (*Love Story*) or 'martyr to the cause' (*When the Bough Breaks*) roles, she was simply so lovely, so endearing, so perfect that she had to be the girl next door. Every mother would like her son to marry her and – as she is quoted as saying – 'And the sons wouldn't have minded either!' She was a star actress whom directors loved to direct; a pleasure for cinematographers to photograph, film crews to work with and the media to interview. Yet in Patricia Roc's case the media should have labelled her a European rose, for she also made films in both France and Italy, and was fluent in both languages.

In the case of Virginia McKenna, there is every reason to have expected the label to have been crushed during her career on the strength of her unglamorous (though appealing) roles, the fact that she suffered a real and well-publicized divorce, and that at one period she had a reputation as our 'British Garbo'. But however tough her films and her lifestyle became, she has somehow always reflected home-loving (especially after *Born Free*) styles which always confirmed the rose stereotype.

It would seem that one British star *did* succeed in totally derosefying herself – although Jean Simmons was helped in her case by Rank, who in 1950 sold the remaining eighteen months of her contract to RKO in the US. She had no say in the deal and was quoted as saying: 'It does seem rather like selling a lump of meat, doesn't it?' After an unhappy start in Hollywood, she ended up as the first real British star to become internationally known in the post-war period. She might well have become more of an English rose than even Deborah Kerr, but love and marriage, Hollywood success and becoming an American citizen ended all that.

These six actresses, here collectively called the English Roses, have made both good and bad British films, and whilst they worked through their careers, under contract, with little choice in the films they made, they battled to hold on to their home and family lives, and in the main they were successful. They took great pride in their achievements, both on and off the screen, and perhaps they should, in the final analysis, be known instead as Rank's Indestructibles.

Whenever Phyllis Calvert tried to retire, events conspired against her and she would find herself back in the cinema limelight. Headlines such as this in 1950: 'A star rebels – no more contracts ... no more personal appearances ... just a home in the country and

Phyllis Calvert in *Madonna of the Seven Moons*, 1944

Virginia McKenna in *Carve her Name with Pride*, 1958

Phyllis Calvert in *Fanny by Gaslight*, 1944

the quiet life', and this in 1953: 'Thought career was over – now top Rank again', are the perfect examples. At the age of thirty-seven, having been away from the screen for three years, she suddenly found herself on the shortlist of the British Film Academy for her performance as the mother of the deaf-mute in the hugely successful *Mandy* (1962). She had stated many times, at the height of her career, that her three ambitions had always been 'a career, a home and family'. And that is exactly what she had achieved and was managing beautifully. She was already becoming what the French called her in 1979 – one of 'les immortels du cinéma'.

Phyllis Calvert was a practical woman who knew her limitations as an actress from the very start, and who had no wish to live at film-star pace. When she was asked how many people she employed in 1950, she commented that it was crazy to have a secretary, a sewing maid, a nanny, a cook and a daily help when she really enjoyed doing it all herself. And that is exactly what she did when her Hollywood period was over.

In 1946 Paramount had offered her a contract stating she had to work for four months of every year for four years. As she left for Tinsel Town she said, 'I shall be back as soon as the film is finished. There'll be trouble for anyone who tries to keep me in America.'

Apart from the US films' lack of success, Phyllis Calvert did not go down well in the world film capital. The *Hollywood Reporter* said: 'Miss Calvert does not seem to have made any study of how she should behave. She is busy being herself.' She admitted to being super-patriotic on the first two visits, as it was just after the War, and the Californians talked endlessly about America's war effort and sacrifices. She couldn't keep quiet and was reported to have let them have it. However, she *was* happy about one set of friendships she made, that of Gary Cooper and his wife. Cooper was the man she had most wanted to meet, but she was told by fellow guests at a party at which he was expected that she wouldn't get very much out of him. He was still a cowboy at heart, she was informed, offering no more than a 'yep' or 'nope'. As it turned out, they got on famously and his wife and Calvert had a great deal in common, including a set of four dresses bought from the same New York fashion house. From then on they would advise each other on what to wear at the endless and obligatory parties that all stars had to attend rather than run the risk at that time of being described as 'doing a Garbo'.

As British audiences were clamouring to see Phyllis Calvert films, the hard-working and loyal contract artist was dreaming of cooking, bottling preserves, weeding the flower-beds, taking her daughter to and from school and just being one of the millions of ordinary mothers and wives living an ordinary life. And it was probably this quality underlying her film persona that made her so attractive to audiences. There was indeed an 'ordinary' quality that simmered beneath the glamorous exterior, to which both male and female cinema-goers could identify and respond. She always played women who were loyal and loving, honest and brave, characteristics that shone in three box-office hits: *The Man in Grey* (1943), *Fanny by Gaslight* (1944) and *Madonna of the Seven Moons* (1944). In these she played, respectively, a warm-hearted innocent wife, the shy adolescent who becomes a powerful woman in the face of adversity, and a saintly wife who disappears to live a few months in blissful amnesia as the lover of a romantic Florentine cut-throat.

Phyllis Calvert was born in 1915, and ten years later began her acting career in Ellen Terry's last play, *Crossings*, at the Lyric, Hammersmith in London – although her film career was completed with *The Walking Stick* in 1970, she still appeared occasionally on stage and in television plays. Quite remarkable for an actress who, after earning two hundred pounds for a day's work at the studio, preferred to be working well after midnight in the garden at home – 'Just for the joy of growing and gathering my own vegetables and flowers.'

Patricia Roc, known as the lovely blonde leading lady of British films in the forties and fifties, would have found little joy in working with vegetables and flowers. She was the most dedicated of the Rank contract actresses at the time, thoughtful and intelligent and with strong views on her film career. She always wanted to try different types of role, though she admitted later that her face was the wrong shape to allow her to play the *femme fatale*. In 1945 *Picturegoer*, the most widely read film magazine in Britain, announced: 'In one film a studio representative admits that Pat Roc was so good in a scene that it had to be cut because she took away sympathy from the heroine and gained it all herself.'

It was said: 'Pat Roc as a private individual is unlike in many ways the girl we know on the screen. Surprisingly sophisticated, she has a quality of glamour which is uncommon in our stars.' It would appear also that she was amazingly genuine and sincere. She was often quoted as hating pretence and posing, which probably accounted for her enormous female fan mail, and her popularity in the studio.

Phyllis Calvert in *Madonna of the Seven Moons*, 1944

In 1945, she was delighted to leave for the US to make *Canyon Passage*, being the first British star to go to Hollywood under the Rank scheme for 'lease-lend' between American and British studios. It was directed by Jacques Tourneur for Universal, and in later years has become a much respected film of the pioneering days in the West. She was the co-star to Dana Andrews, supported by a strong cast that included Brian Donlevy, Hoagy Carmichael and Susan Hayward. However, at the time it had no box-office success either in the US or England, and nor did a second American film, *The Man on the Eiffel Tower* (1950). Patricia Roc's British career continued successfully until 1953, at which time she settled in Paris and gave birth to a son whose father was a leading French cameraman, André Thomas. Her son was actually born two months after she'd left her husband, and by 1954 she was in Rome and filming. By the time she returned to England she had made at least eight films in France and Italy, but her career, apart from two poorly received films, *The Hypnotist* (1957) and *Bluebeard's Ten Honeymoons* (1960), had come to an end.

Patricia Roc really was one of England's best film talents and the most beautiful faces in films in the 1940s. She was born in 1918 in London, her father a Dutchman born in Belgium, and her mother half Spanish, half French. She was educated in London and Paris, and adored French films – 'what French film is not worthwhile?' she once remarked. In a five-year period (1943–7) she made twelve major films, including *Millions Like Us* (1943), *Love Story* (1944), *Madonna of the Seven Moons* (1944), *The Wicked Lady* (1945) and in 1947 she was making three films at the same time – *Jassy*, *The Brothers*, (her favourite film) and *So Well Remembered*. The following year she made *When the Bough Breaks* (1948), playing the star part in a daring film of the time concerning bigamy.

The quality of Patricia Roc's performances stand the test of time, although she has always maintained that her British films have no great claims on her. As she set herself such high standards she was at times in conflict with Rank over her contract. She cared about the films she made and questioned the insistence on an unquestioning willingness to appear in any picture on the production schedule. There was never open warfare or contract breaking, just constant tension and the threat of a 'difficult star' with a talent ahead of her time.

An actress who could never have been considered 'difficult', and who unquestionably was the star of the 1940s, is Margaret Lockwood. She had, on average, 5,000 fan letters a week, and there were huge queues at the box office wherever her films played, and yet her talent seemed to be difficult for her critics (and there were many) to understand. Whenever she made a good picture, they would heap their praise on the directors and screenwriters; when she starred in a bad film, then Margaret Lockwood was blamed. One critic reviewing *Cardboard Cavalier* (1948), where she made a change of style to comedy which was not a success, wrote: 'A custard pie in Lockwood's face was not particularly funny, but I did find it very satisfying.'

Cinema highbrows dismissed her as having no personality and lacking the appeal of foreign stars. Producers claimed she couldn't act, and a spokesman for Rank when they finally closed down their 'Charm School' stated that they couldn't *even* find another Lockwood. Yet twenty million paid at the box office to watch Margaret Lockwood in one of the most popular films of the War years, *Love Story* (1944). She played a pianist who has only a few months to live, and on wind-swept cliff-tops, against romantic piano music, she has a passionate affair with a man who is going blind. Then in 1946 she played the outrageous, murderous highwaywoman 'Lady Skelton' in *The Wicked Lady*, and over thirty million paid more than a million pounds to see it. No Hollywood female star – not even Garbo at that stage – had created such figures for film-makers. Not bad results for a girl who couldn't act.

She was born in Karachi, her father being the chief superintendent on India's North-West Railway, and when she was two years old she arrived in England. At thirteen she made her stage debut as a 'babe' in *Babes In The Wood*, at the Scala Theatre in London, and then proceeded to appear in cabarets and 'tea dances' before she enrolled simultaneously at RADA and a school of dancing. It would seem that the seeds of workaholism were planted at a very early age. She did indeed thrive on work: it was said that if you wandered into Rank's three leading ladies' dressing rooms you would probably find shopping lists and things for the home in Phyllis Calvert's, make-up and beautiful clothes in Patricia Roc's, and in Margaret Lockwood's there would only be her latest script and a photograph of her daughter.

She had a compulsion and talent for work. By the time she first concentrated on her film career, she had been in numerous theatre

successes in the West End. In 1937 she made her film presence felt with a touching portrayal of the nurse in Carol Reed's Bank Holiday, and consequently Hitchcock immediately cast her as lead in *The Lady Vanishes* (1938), in which she presented a true and sympathetic personality – probably the key to the positive audience reaction when she later played her 'wicked' roles. She was whisked off to Hollywood, but, like her close friend Phyllis Calvert, she had no wish to settle in the film capital.

Marriage, a daughter (whom she nicknamed 'Toots') and votes as top female actress for three consecutive – 1946, 1947 and 1948 – nationwide polls sponsored by the *Daily Mail* turned her into a lasting star. The film which started the adulation was *The Man in Grey* (1943), in which she played the scheming mistress of her best friend's husband, who allows her best friend to die from pneumonia before finally being whipped to death by her furious lover. Then in 1945 *The Wicked Lady* amazed and delighted both film-makers and audiences. She said at the time: 'The public adores the stuff ... we never had any location shooting on *The Man in Grey* or *The Wicked Lady*. A couple of strategically placed trees and a plant or two, stuck in the studio, made a forest, and nobody asks questions.' Not so the critics. She was dismayed by the critical reaction (Birmingham City Council banned it as 'too unhealthy for Sunday viewing') and her producers panicked after reviews on the day of the Royal première to be attended by Queen Mary. Although she was known publicly as a broad-minded woman, should she be allowed to attend? Representatives were called from Marlborough House to see it, and they passed it fit for a queen. In fact it subsequently became one of Queen Mary's favourite films, and she often showed it privately to friends.

below, Margaret Lockwood and Patricia Roc in *The Wicked Lady*, 1945

below right, Margaret Lockwood in *Love Story*, 1944

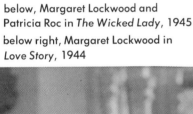

Margaret Lockwood was a film phenomenon; she was also a 'trouper' and a natural performer. She would finish a film, rehearse a new play, pack her bags, load the car with luggage and 'Toots' and drive off to tour the provinces. She'd soon be back filming and looking forward to a stint of Peter Pan at the Scala.

Margaret Lockwood was a star who always had something more than a pretty face and a permanent beauty mark on her cheek. She was no ordinary girl who appealed to all other ordinary girls. She could act. And even though she suffered in private over the slings and arrows thrown at her by the media, she never let it show in public. She once threw this exit-line at a group of critics who were invited to a film preview and to meet her afterwards: 'Goodbye, it was nice to be among friends, even though they aren't mine.'

Virginia McKenna, in her autobiography, states that 'some of my best friends have tails'. That's just as well, because her studio and her critics turned their backs on the girl who was called 'the original English rose of English films'. By 1962 her film career was at a standstill, and even after she had played gritty, unglamorous roles in *Simba* (1955), *A Town Like Alice* (1956) and *Carve Her Name with Pride* (1958), references to the delicate flower were still being made. The media at this time continually informed the public that Virginia McKenna was a recluse with her husband Bill Travers, and that the Rank contract actress, who had won the Best Actress of the Year award for her performance in *A Town Like Alice* and had such rave reviews as Violette Szabo in *Carve Her Name with Pride*, the first woman to win the George Cross for her courage as an agent in occupied France, was now unlikely to make another film. Was she 'doing another Garbo'? Nobody could get close enough to find out.

Anyway, she did make another film, the huge success *Born Free* (1966), and she followed this with seven more, five of them with animals in featured roles! *Born Free* happened at a time when she needed to be free herself, away from film contracts and the disciplined life of film-making. It is doubtful whether this surprisingly good British actress realized that the caring and

above left, Margaret Lockwood in *I'll be Your Sweetheart*, 1945

above, Virginia McKenna in *A Town Like Alice*, 1956

below, Jean Simmons and David Tomlinson in *So Long at the Fair*, 1950

above right, Margaret Lockwood and Patricia Roc in *The Wicked Lady*, 1945

right, Stewart Granger, Margaret Lockwood and Patricia Roc in *Love Story*, 1944

below right, Virginia McKenna in *Carve Her Name with Pride*, 1958

campaigning for wildlife was going to become more important to her than her career. For up until that point in her life she had, as she put it, 'worked hard, had no family ties, made a few good pictures, as well as a few ghastly ones, and thoroughly enjoyed it all'.

She came from an interesting family background – her great-uncle Reginald McKenna the Liberal statesman of the Edwardian era, her great-grandfather Sir Morrell Mackenzie a famous throat specialist, and her brother Stephen McKenna the novelist – and she had a sharp mind. She was born in 1931, of an actress and cabaret pianist who was half French and half Scottish. Virginia McKenna studied drama and went into repertory theatre in Dundee, and had experience in television before making her first film in 1952. Then in 1953 she played the young Wren Julie (the 'glamour pants at op') in *The Cruel Sea*, an unrelenting and wonderfully made war film. She was now a Rank contract artist and on her way to some exciting leading film roles. At this time her career meant a great deal to her, and the good parts she was given took their emotional toll. Parts that other actresses longed for, were harrowing and traumatic for Virginia McKenna to play. On *Carve Her Name With Pride*, Odette Hallowes, GC, MBE, *Légion d'honneur* (who in 1950 had her own biography *Odette* filmed, which detailed her career as an agent for the British in war-torn France and her capture and torture at the hands of the Nazis) was the technical adviser, and she worked closely with McKenna. She stated later to the press: 'Virginia has the same strong will, she could have been one of us. She has courage and a mind of her own. If you've been through it you can judge the mentality of the right people, and a woman knows things about another woman.'

Virginia McKenna always believed that it is only through loving someone or something that there can be any perspective in life. Through her family, which at one stage included a husband, four children, four dogs, a cat, two rabbits, twelve tropical fish, four goldfish, a visiting squirrel and a prematurely-born deer, and through her later films which included Elsa the lioness in *Born Free*, Tarka the otter in *Ring of Bright Water* (1969), Slowly in *An Elephant Called Slowly* (1970) and Christian in *Christian the Lion* (1976), she found perspective in her work as a film actress as well.

Jean Simmons knows only too well what it is like to live on the land and be surrounded by wildlife. At the time her film career was taking shape, she was married to Stewart Granger and owned a 10,000-acre ranch in Tucson, Arizona and a 70,000-acre ranch in

Jean Simmons in *Blue Lagoon*, 1949

Silver City, New Mexico, where she spent her time surrounded by cattle. It would appear that although she was content at times with her Wild West living style, she was much happier in homes around Hollywood. Like the one looking out to the Santa Monica mountains; this was her Californian mountain eyrie with the cricket-bat window pane, where once had lived the actor and former Sussex cricketer, Sir C. Aubrey Smith.

Born in 1929, this beautiful and talented British actress made her first film at fourteen, when she was chosen from a group of dance students to play Margaret Lockwood's younger sister in *Give Us the Moon*. At 5.30 on a fateful Friday 13 August, 1943, she was interviewed amongst 200 other hopefuls, and by 6.30, without a screen-test, her Rank contract was signed. This was the end of her dancing dreams, and by the time she was seventeen she had achieved stardom. From 1946 to 1953 she made at least two films a year for Rank, and her roles included the spoiled young Estella in David Lean's *Great Expectations* (1946), the native girl infatuated by Sabu in *Black Narcissus* (1947), the ship-wrecked child in *Blue Lagoon* (1949), and in the same year a delightful performance as the young orphan who takes Stewart Granger as her father in *Adam and Evelyne*. In 1948 Laurence Olivier had chosen her to play Ophelia in his filming of Shakespeare's *Hamlet*. Her performance won her Best Actress awards in Europe and she was nominated for an Oscar. When she was seventeen, the film capital had already acknowleged her talent.

Jean Simmons was a graceful and delicate beauty, and of all the actresses mentioned in these pages could have been considered to be the most perfect of roses. But as her performances and films were so varied, and because Hollywood captured her at such an early stage in her life and career, the dreaded two words were never linked to her. Unlike most of her fellow Brits, Hollywood, after a miserable start, suited her well. She arrived in 1950, sold by Rank to Howard Hughes's RKO, by 1953 she had freed herself in

above, Jean Simmons in *Adam and Evelyne*, 1949

top right, Jean Simmons in *Adam and Evelyne*, 1949

right, Deborah Kerr in *I See a Dark Stranger*, 1945

below, Jean Simmons in *Trottie True*, 1949

Deborah Kerr in *Black Narcissus*, 1947

the courts from the legal binds of the Hughes contract and at last, at the age of twenty-four, her career could fly internationally.

Stewart Granger, on meeting her for the first time when working on *Caesar and Cleopatra* (1945), referred to her as 'a scruffy little rat'. Jean Simmons's reply to the press was, 'I got a terrible pash on him. I also got his autograph.' There always seemed to be a genuinely innocent and vulnerable quality about her, and for this reason in most of her roles she would always be on the side of the angels.

As far as Deborah Kerr (Kerr rhymes with star) was concerned, audiences around the world believed she *was* an angel. She was born in Scotland in 1921, won a scholarship to the Sadler's Wells Ballet School, and at seventeen made her London début in the *corps de ballet* of *Prometheus*. She soon realized her frame was a bit bulky, and felt it was her face that she would have to work with. Director Michael Powell noticed her in her agent's office and decided to write a little part into *Contraband* (1940) for 'a plump little dumpling who was obviously going places'. The 'little part' was eventually cut, and it was a swan (who grew out of the dumpling) that was spotted by producer Gabriel Pascal, who in fact walked up to her in a restaurant and called her a 'sweet virgin'. He cast her as a Salvation Army lass to be slapped around by Robert Newton in *Major Barbara* 1941). She slapped so photogenically that four more films followed within the next twelve months. Then, in 1942, Michael Powell cast his 'little dumpling' again in *The Life and Death of Colonel Blimp*, and a new star was discovered. In this film she played three archetypes of English womanhood – a governess circa 1900, a country-family débutante in the 1920s, and an Army Corps girl in the Second World War.

She was good, but she was even more impressive in colour. Deborah Kerr's natural colouring would have given Renoir a fit of the shakes. In Technicolor she was stunningly beautiful. Metro British were immediately determined to capture this new face, and MGM in Hollywood were alerted. Three films later she was on her way to America, with a contract that raised the film industry's temperature – seven years at $3,000 a week, no options, and she was to be starred or co-starred in all films.

Two of the films she made before leaving for a new life and, like Jean Simmons, an international career, were a clever and modestly made comedy-thriller about Nazi spies in Ireland called *I See a Dark Stranger* (1946) (in which the leading part was specially written for her) and then back to Technicolor in the striking and at times memorable *Black Narcissus* (1947). Oscars were awarded for both the art-design and colour photography. Set in the Himalayas, it was all shot in Surrey, with Deborah Kerr playing the first of her several nun roles.

Hollywood now owned a 'romantic Englishwoman', and much to her relief they were careful not to change her image. She loved her life in the film capital, and she looked forward to a host of fine films. She has stated many times that being at MGM was like being a member of a very special club. Indeed, it was a special club, and through being a member she was nominated for a Best Actress Oscar six times.

Deborah Kerr has remained a star throughout her screen career. In fact she admits that she was an instant star, and worked to become a fine actress. As governesses, nuns, one nymphomaniac and one alcoholic; as anguished wives and mothers, and more governesses and nuns she has made world audiences laugh and cry and made them forget at times that she was ever an English rose. Recently, when asked what she would like film historians to say about her she replied quickly, 'I would like them to say I was not an English rose.'

A request that would have the very real sympathy of five other fine British actresses.

4

Leave 'Em Laughing

There can be little doubt that in the beginning British film comedy was merely an extension of music-hall and variety-theatre comedy sketches. Indeed, all the sucessful early film comedians came solely from this background. Many years later, actors who where referred to as 'legitimate' – implying that performers from music-hall backgrounds were illegitimate – began to take over, and instead of comedy films being just vehicles for vaudevillians to perform their old routines, they began to be scripted in much the same manner as dramas. The public, as it became more sophisticated, demanded as much of the scenario as of the participants, always allowing, of course, for sequences where a speciality spot could be slotted in, and where an established comedian could perform a routine or variation on one that had taken many years of 'treading the boards' to perfect.

By combining well-plotted storylines with countless opportunities for gags and comedy 'business', film funny men could draw the laughter-hungry public, anxious to get away from the dreariness of the factory floor, office or shop counter, into the one-and-nines for a damned good belly laugh – a better tonic than any doctor could prescribe. The men – for they were principally men – who made up this select band of box-office film comedians were as varied in style and appearance as the audiences who came to see them. And in the first days of comedy talkies – the early 1930s – these audiences were fiercely loyal to their funny men. There were low-budget comedy films featuring performers that would pack the cinemas in the north of England, and empty them in the south, and vice versa. This was just not due to difficulties in understanding dialect; it was more the fundamental difference in geographical areas, where taste in humour is almost parochial.

Today, largely because of television networks, such comedy borderlines have become somewhat blurred, and yet there are still some big-fee-earning comedians who can get solid bookings for months in clubs north of Watford, but couldn't, as they would be the first to admit, 'get arrested' when they step south of the border. And so it was in the comedy film heyday of such men as Frank Randle. Fortunately many northern comedians, unlike good wine, travelled well; perhaps George Formby was the best example. His light, simple style and, perhaps even more, his light-fingered dexterity on the ukulele with his catchy little ditties, made him a national but certainly not an international film star. On a more cerebral comedy level than Formby and from even further north, there entered the film-fun scene a man who is rightly regarded as one of the greatest British screen comedians of all time. His name – Will Hay.

Will Hay in *Oh Mr Porter*, 1938

Jack Hulbert in *Jack's the Boy*, 1932

46

Hay was born in Aberdeen in December, 1888, and like Britain's first comedian to aspire to a knighthood, Sir George Robey – the self-styled 'Prime Minister of Mirth' – he quit a 'respectable' career in engineering to enter the entertainment industry. After beginning in an Isle of Man concert party, Will Hay slowly climbed the showbiz spiral staircase to become one of the best sketch comedians on the halls. He achieved permanent fame with his caracature of a schoolmaster trying to teach the boys in his class, who were virtually all much smarter than he was, so that only by fumbling and bluffing his way through the lesson was he able just about to keep control. 'Where was the Magna Carta signed?' 'Why ... er ... why, above the dotted line of course!' Sketches of this nature require split-second timing, but Hay had that ability in abundance, and he was able to use it to greater effect than any of his contemporaries.

Hay's smooth transition from stage to screen was probably so successful because he was the first comic to realize that film comedy had to be performed with far more nuances than on the 'halls'. He also realized the importance of strong characterization, of good straight-acting support, and above all of the plausibility of the storyline. It was with the writers Marriot Edgar, Van Guest and J.O.C. Horton and the director Marcel Varnel that Will Hay made some of the funniest comedy films ever produced in Britain. Films such as the classic *Oh Mr Porter* (1938), with Hay as the incompetent station-master, Moore Marriott, the toothless old 'Harbottle' and Graham Moffatt – fat boy 'Albert' (two of Hay's most notable foils). It rates in most film *aficionados*' opinion as the top British screen comedy of the 1930s. Following this, with the same team, and almost equal in success, came *Convict 99* (1938), *Old Bones of the River* (1938) and *Ask a Policeman* (1939). The *Motion Picture Herald* listed Hay among the top ten British box-office stars. Few film comedians of that era aspired to that sort of status.

Will Hay had two show-business personas. The first was as a solo

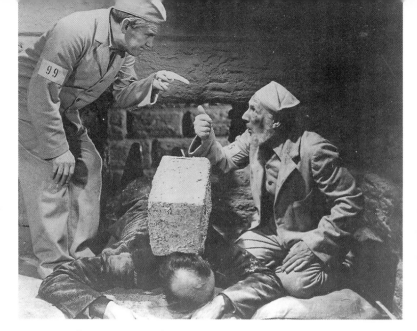

artiste, often compared to W.C. Fields, the great American comedian, for his arrogant and yet inadvertently self-deprecating style, and because both men were very competent jugglers. The second was as the leader of a zany film team which was often regarded as the British equivalent to the Marx Brothers.

Will Hay was a reticent man, his private life was very precious to him, and he rarely gave press interviews. He was a genuine intellectual and made several appearances on the BBC's *Brains Trust*. He was an air fanatic and a highly respected astronomer – his greatest achievement in this field was in 1933, when he discovered the large white spot on Saturn. He was later to write a book on the subject, *Through My Telescope*, which was reprinted and used to good effect as an official training manual by the Home Guard in the Second World War. Hay's personal contribution to the war effort was to join the Navy, and as a sub-Lieutenant in the RNVR's Special Branch, he instructed the Sea Cadet Corps in astronomy and navigation. As well as continuing to make hilarious feature films during the War, Hay made a highly entertaining and informative documentary called *Go to Blazes*, directed by that comedy veteran Walter Forde, which told in amusing terms how to deal with incendiary bombs.

In 1943, whilst making what was to be his last film – a comedy send-up of the legal profession, *My Learned Friend*, Hay became ill, and the early stages of cancer were diagnosed. Thereafter, for the remaining years of his life, he confined his talents almost exclusively to radio. He finally succumbed to the illness in April 1949. Will Hay will always be remembered in the hall of fame as the man who did more than most other British film comedians to bring to the screen a serious approach to comedy. He never regarded himself as a true comedian, just a character actor looking for those human frailties which we can all recognize and are able to laugh at. This, coupled with his mastery of comic timing, is the reason Will Hay's films have so steadily withstood the test of time, and remain as funny today as ever.

above left, Will Hay in *Convict 99*, 1938

above, Will Hay in *Ask a Policeman*, 1938

below, Sid Field in *London Town*, 1947

The word 'genius' has all too often been bandied about in the world of entertainment. In the field of film comedy, it has fortunately been used more sparingly. Clearly, some exponents of this most elusive and exacting art form richly deserve such labelling – Charlie Chaplin, Stan Laurel, Buster Keaton, Jack Benny, Max Miller, Max Wall, Tony Hancock and George Burns among them. But high up on the list of these comedy greats, one would have to add the name of Sid Field, the man who claimed, with doleful irony, that it took him thirty years to become an overnight star.

Sid Field was born in Birmingham on April Fool's day 1904, and he began his love affair with comedy when, as a small boy, he dressed up in his father's trousers, boots and wing collar to give backyard impersonations of Chaplin. Later, when searching for a wider audience than a couple of other small boys and a line full of washing, he ventured one day into the street and caused chaos among the traffic. He was then hauled back by the ear to his home by a bobby on the beat and told, 'We've already got one Chaplin, we don't need any more', a statement that Field would one day totally disprove. He began his professional career in a juvenile troupe with three other boys and ten minx-like little girls – the Royal Kino Juveniles. He was eleven years old at the time. After twenty-eight years of touring the halls, progressing from comedy feed, song-and-dance man, light comedian to laughter-maker without any gimmicks except talent, Sid finally found himself in the West End of London in a show called *Strike a New Note*.

The show opened at the Prince of Wales Theatre in 1943. At the time of the first performance, there was not one single 'name' artist on the bill. In the programme there was a very prophetic footnote, however. 'Here is youth', it declared. Although Sid at the age of thirty-nine would have been the first to admit that he neither felt, nor for that matter looked, youthful. The note went on: 'All are players of experience, needing but the opportunity to make themselves known.' Sid Field was to become not just known, but positively acclaimed by the public. In less than three weeks, the theatre posters were changed to read 'Sid Field' – the new funny man'. After all those years of obscurity, Sid Field had arrived, and theatre critics began asking where this genius had come from, where had he been hiding! They would merely have had to take a short hop on the bus to North London just six weeks before to find the answer, because at the Finsbury Park Empire he had been doing virtually the same act in front of a tough and far less enthusiastic audience.

Nevertheless, Field's sketches rightly rate among the all-time theatre comedy classics – 'The Golf Lesson', 'The Photographer', the post-war spiv 'Slasher Green' are little masterpieces. His comedy was the pure old gold of music hall, with a simple situation set against a simple background on which he would build layer upon layer of laughter. Fortunately some of his greatest sketches have been preserved in glorious Technicolor in the film *London Town* (1946). In this million-dollar musical fiasco, which lost its way in direction as well as its mammoth budget, Sid's sketches glitter like

diamonds in a base metal setting.

Two years later he made his last feature film, this time as a Cromwellian barrow boy in *Cardboard Cavalier*. It has to be said that the screen never totally captured his special brand of mirthful magic, but in the two films he made that were released by Rank, there are some marvellous moments of comedy timing and 'business', that rate alongside any produced by his idol, Charlie Chaplin.

Tragically, Sid Field's bright starlight shone all too briefly. A mere six years after he had 'made it', he died of a heart attack when he was only forty-five. Kenneth Tynan, the renowned theatre critic, wryly observed that 'alcohol and self criticism were his pall bearers'. He is sadly missed, not just by an adoring public which, when remembering him, will find a smile has crept across its face, but also by so many of today's well-established big-name comedians, whose approach to comedy and style he influenced so powerfully.

There was a stylish silver-voiced link between Sid Field and Norman Wisdom, their comedy 'feed' Jerry Desmonde. Jerry, whose real name was James Robert Sadler, at first joined Sid in 1942, and he was so good that audiences watching the famous golf or photographer sketch, could be forgiven at times if they believed it was a double act. When Sid had so unexpectedly made his last exit, Norman Wisdom was quick off the mark to persuade Jerry to become his straight man, and it was a masterful move. If Jerry was Sid's right-hand man, he was most certainly Norman's left-hand man. Norman and Jerry were as important to early-1950s British film fun as Bud Abbott and Lou Costello were for American cinema audiences in the 1940s, and the similarities did not stop there either. Not so much, perhaps in appearance. Wisdom is small and wiry. Costello was small but tubby. It was their straight men who bore comparison. Bud Abbott was slim, persuasive and aggressive, while Jerry Desmonde was tall, angular and also persuasive and aggressive, but in a more refined English way.

Wisdom, like Chaplin, leaned heavily on the 'plight of the little man against the world' approach to comedy, and also like Chaplin he resorted, sometimes too often for comfort, to winning over audiences by the old clown ploy of pathos. He was, nevertheless, the most successful British film comedian in the traditional sense since the Second World War, and his films – particularly those crafted by screen-writer Jack Davies, who had learned all the tricks of the trade, along with Marriott Edgar and Val Guest, writing side-splitting scenarios for Will Hay – testify to that success.

Norman Wisdom was born in 1918, and started the musical side of his life as an Army bandsman, later taking the familiar route of touring 'the halls' to hone and polish his act. When he first appeared 'live' on the one channel, BBC television, his impact on audiences was immediate. He was described by critics as the new Chaplin. In 1953 he made his film début as the star of *Trouble in Store* a film where the comedy relied mainly on well-constructed and lengthy slapstick routines. The formula was employed in all of his most memorable film comedies: *The Square Peg* in 1958; and perhaps his funniest, *On the Beat* in 1962 and *A Stitch in Time*, made a year later.

Norman Wisdom, although far less active in films and television these days, is still a major theatre draw, and whenever he does make one of his rare appearances, he can be certain of a packed house, and an audience which almost knows his routines as well as he does, and yet still loves every minute of them.

below, Norman Wisdom in *On the Beat*, 1962

below right, Sid Field and Jerry Desmond in *London Town*, 1947

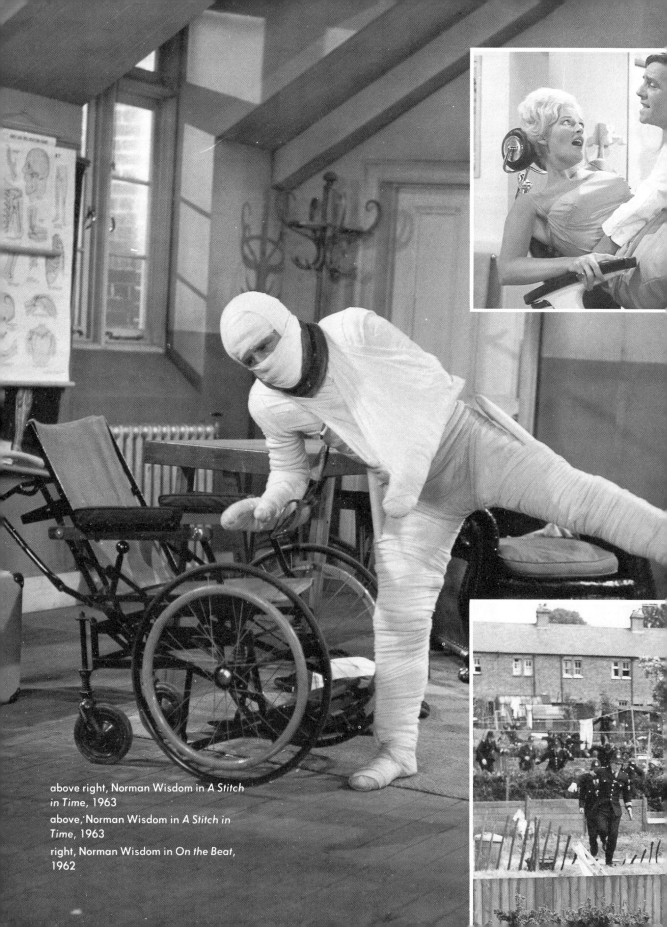

above right, Norman Wisdom in *A Stitch in Time*, 1963

above, Norman Wisdom in *A Stitch in Time*, 1963

right, Norman Wisdom in *On the Beat*, 1962

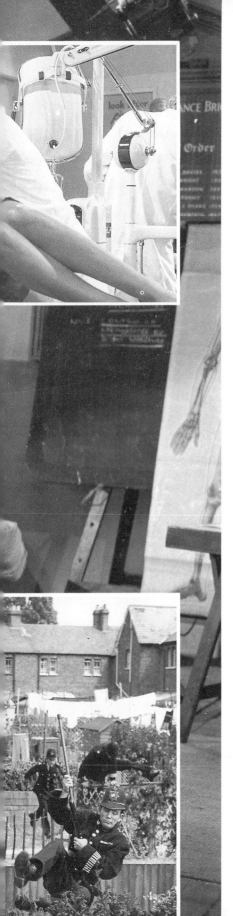

Arthur Askey in *The Ghost Train*, 1941

In the same 'little man' mould as Wisdom, but a comic who had made his mark through the medium of radio many years before Wisdom became a star, was Arthur Askey. Askey was a native of Liverpool which was then and to a certain extent is today, a fertile breeding ground for comedians: Ted Ray, Ken Dodd, Tommy Handley, Jimmy Tarbuck and a whole host of other top British funny men learned their craft in this great cosmopolitan seaport city. Arthur began his comedy career in a concert party, and for fourteen years appeared at end-of-the-pier shows, cracking gags, singing his silly little songs (like the 'Busy Bee' song, which he always performed with freshness that made it seem as though it was being sung for the first time) and doing pier-type dance routines.

In January 1938, he made his first radio broadcast with his long-time foil, Richard 'Stinker' Murdoch, in a show called *Band Waggon*. It was, for its day, a very innovative idea, and it worked on the premiss that Arthur and Dickie were squatters (although that term was not in general use then) in a small flat on the top of Broadcasting House. Keeping them company up on the roof were a whole menagerie of animals, Lewis the goat, Hector the camel, and pigeons named Lucy and Basil. The show, which poked fun at the BBC was at first show to capture a big audience, but soon Arthur's catch-phrases 'Ay thang-yew' and 'Hello, playmates' became part of everyday street conversation, and *Band Waggon* was a national hit. It was the forerunner and format-setter of nearly all of Britain's classic comedy radio shows, from *ITMA* to the *Goon Show* to *Hancock's Half-Hour*.

It was such a success, in fact, that a film was made using the same title and idea, and this led to a film career for Askey that went from the late 1930s well into the 1950s. Most notable of the films were *Charley's Big-hearted Aunt* (1940), *The Ghost Train* (1941), *King Arthur Was a Gentleman* (1942), *The Love Match* (1954) and *Friends and Neighbours* (1959). The diminutive Arthur more than made up in laughs for all the hard years of struggle he had had to take him to the top. He was 'big-hearted' in every sense of the' phrase and, like all the comedians recalled in this chapter, a genuine original.

The Crazy Gang in *Gasbags*, 1940

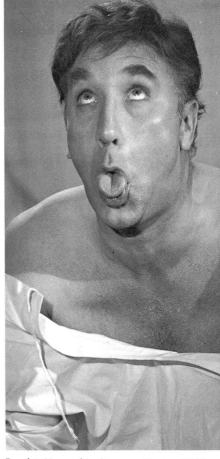
Frankie Howerd in *Carry on Doctor*, 1968

In 1932, the impresario George Black tried an experimental week at the London Palladium. He called it 'Crazy Week', and the basis of the show was to link together three well-known provincial comedy double acts, and a comedy juggler. They were Nervo and Knox, Naughton and Gold, Caryll and Mundy, representing the cross-patter duos, and Eddie Gray, with his handlebar moustache, fractured French and Indian clubs as the solo juggler. All of the acts got involved with each other in 'impromptu' running gags and slapstick routines – and the audience loved it.

'Crazy Week' was extended to a month, another double act, called Flanagan and Allen, replaced Caryll and Mundy, and the Crazy Gang was born. As they say in showbiz, the show ran and ran, and *March Hares* was the beginning of a whole series of separate, individually titled, riotous revues for the team, who became a national institution. They were the favourite mirth-makers of the Royal Family, and just about everyone else. Soon their exploits were to be seen on the screen and the same team that made such a success of the Will Hay film comedies, director Marcel Varnel and comedy writers Marriott Edgar and Val Guest, were responsible for such hits as *Alf's Button Afloat* (1938), *The Frozen Limits* (1939) and the wartime farce *Gasbags* (1940). It was the War that rudely interrupted their Palladium season, and when it ended in 1945, Val Parnell, who was now in charge of booking for the theatre, thought that the 'Gang' might no longer have the drawing power that they had previously enjoyed. He could not have been more wrong, and when Jack Hylton presented them at a new venue – the Victoria Palace – they proved more popular than ever. They made only one more film together after the War, *Life is a Circus* (1954), but their spontaneity and their impish sense of fun could never really be captured fully on film, even though they made some very amusing ones. The stage was their true *métier*, a live audience their meat and drink.

Sid James and Hattie Jacques in *Carry on Loving*, 1970

What the Crazy Gang were to the London stage, the 'Carry On' team were to the British cinema and, like the Crazy Gang, they too had a run that spanned three decades. The 'Carry On' films began with a low-budget comedy on the Army in 1958 called *Carry on Sergeant*. After that, almost two a year were made right up until 1978. Titles such as *Carry on Nurse*, *Carry on at Your Convenience*, *Carry on Loving* and *Carry on up the Khyber* became as much a part of British cinema as the girl in the spotlight with the ice cream tray, the organist rising from the pit on the wurlitzer with its flashing coloured lights, and the house manager in his immaculate evening suit.

All of the 'Carry On' films were in the very confident hands of two fine film craftsmen, Peter Rogers, the producer, and Gerald Thomas, the director. Peter Rogers's own background was steeped in film comedy, beginning in 1942 when he worked as a writer, continuing as co-producer during the 1940s and early 1950s. It was this invaluable experience which gave him the uncanny knack of gauging just what the British public wanted in terms of film fun – a mixture of farce, innuendo, lots of scantily clad girls with ample proportions, and a cast of very professional buffoons. The plots had to be a vehicle for all of these ingredients, and scriptwriter Talbot Rothwell kept the stories and the gags bubbling over, even making the old chestnuts seem appetizing enough for a serving of fresh laughter. Gerald Thomas had begun his directing career on a more serious note, with excellent thrillers such as *Time Lock* and *Vicious Circle*. His comedy touch came to the fore when he directed a relative newcomer to films, rock n' roll singer Tommy Steele, in *The Duke Wore Jeans* (1958). In that same year he began the first of the 'Carry On' films, and he carried on directing all of them till the final curtain.

Kenneth Connor in *Carry on Girls*, 1974

Although there were variations in the personnel of the team, the principal participants remained very much the same. They were splendid comedy character actors rather than variety comedians, stalwarts such as Sid James, Kenneth Williams, Kenneth Connor, Hattie Jacques, Bernard Bresslaw, Joan Sims, Barbara Windsor and Jim Dale being the artistes who made the most consistent appearances.

The 'Carry On' films have been dismissed by many critics as crude and trivial but, as someone once said, 'No one ever built a statue to a critic', and these films are now gaining a whole new audience of dedicated young followers who watch them on television and video, elevating some of the best of them to cult status. The 'Carry On' films have a permanent place in history of the British cinema, and rightly so, for they have brought saucy harmless fun in an animated seaside-postcard way to millions of cinema-goers. British comedy film-makers have always gone straight to the funny bone, knowing full well that, unlike so many other countries, Britain has this unique sense of humour in which it is able to laugh heartily at itself. It is a highly prized national characteristic, and long may it live.

top left, Sid James in *Carry on Up the Khyber*, 1969

left, Joan Sims in *Carry on Up the Khyber*, 1969

5

I Spy

S pies are real people. They have always existed, gnawing away at the tatters of society, like ticks on the underbelly of an elephant. The cinema has always exploited our knowledge that they are around ... somewhere. John Buchan once said about his writing: 'Events defy probability, but march just inside possibility.' With those eight words, he had summed up the secret of spy films. Their mixture of the commonplace with the extraordinary, the ease with which laughs turn into thrills, the way a coded secret can suddenly mean life or death for a group of innocent people.

Little wonder then, that *The Lady Vanishes* continues to remain such a favourite for cinema-goers. It is a mystery, a thriller, a comedy and a romance, all entwined round a plot involving spies and coded military secrets. With a beautiful heroine, an appealing hero and a train packed full of eccentrics, we cannot but enjoy the perfect blend of thrills and comedy.

Alfred Hitchcock's classic original version of *The Lady Vanishes*, made in 1938, quickly became established as one of the best-loved films of his career. Strangely enough, it was only by chance that Hitchcock was involved with the film at all. Being at the height of his success, Hitchcock was allowed to work on any project he liked. His usual, meticulous method was to find a story and then develop and supervise the project from this initial idea. But at this time he was unable to find anything that interested him. It was Edward Black of Gainsborough Studios who suggested to Hitchcock a screenplay written by Sidney Gilliat and Frank Launder based on the novel by Ethel L. White, *The Wheel Spins*. The film had first been planned back in 1936 when American director Roy William Neil had been signed to make it. Some location work had actually begun in Yugoslavia during August of that year under the supervision of assistant director Fred Gunn. But unfortunately Gunn fractured an ankle, and whilst he was in hospital the local police managed to get hold of a script. They thought the content was derogatory to their country and immediately had the entire crew thrown into jail before unceremoniously deporting them back to England. In contrast, Hitchcock never even contemplated going abroad for location shots on *The Lady Vanishes*. The entire production was filmed in five weeks on a ninety-foot sound stage at Islington.

During the filming, Hitchcock was playing his usual practical jokes. One of his favourite ploys was to get out a stopwatch, which he used to try and intimidate the actors. Derrick de Marney wrote about this, whilst working with Hitchcock on *Young And Innocent* in 1937: 'Hitch rushed Nova Pilbeam and myself through the first scene and when "cut" was called he appeared to be sleeping. Then

Margaret Lockwood and Dame May Whitty in *The Lady Vanishes*, 1938

Naunton Wayne, Basil Radford and Linden Travers in *The Lady Vanishes*, 1938

he opened his eyes wearily, looked at his stopwatch and said, ... "Too slow. I had that scene marked for thirty seconds and you took fifty. We'll have to re-take the scene.'"

Despite such tricks, *The Lady Vanishes* greatly benefits from the apparent ease and charm of the performances. Margaret Lockwood has just the right amount of vulnerability and toughness, whilst Michael Redgrave (in his film début) brings out the full humour of a script brimming with sharp, witty lines, in a style that would later win him awards. And in the supporting roles, Basil Radford and Naunton Wayne, giving their first incarnation as the cricket-obsessed Charters and Caldicott, and the incomparable Dame May Whitty as the mysterious Miss Froy, have gone down in film history. The film is not without its *longueurs* today; but its good-naturedness is eventually winning.

When *The Lady Vanishes* was finally released, it was a triumphant success. In America the New York film critics and the *New York Times* voted it Best Film of the year, and Alfred Hitchcock was firmly established as the premier thriller director of his generation.

above right, Oscar Hamolka in
Sabotage, 1938

It is understandable, therefore that there was some resistance and a great deal of difficulty involved in persuading people that a re-make of *The Lady Vanishes* was worth considering. It was first planned as a feature for American television starring George C. Scott and Candice Bergen, with the idea of having it set aboard a train from Chicago to Los Angeles, and a plot that brought things into the present day and involved the Mafia. The producers then reverted to the original script, but it was only with the financial muscle of Rank that it finally got under way, with Elliott Gould and Cybill Shepherd starring. We can be thankful it did. The new version of *The Lady Vanishes* is as good as, and in some ways better than, the Hitchcock version. There is suspense, but it never gets too serious. How could it? The story is ridiculous. Why should a little old granny be used as a top spy, and why would the secrets be coded in the tune of a folksong? As Hitchcock said of the plot: 'The first thing I throw out is logic.'

By contrast *Sabotage* (1936) is probably one of Hitchcock's most disturbing films. On the original English release, critics and public alike were shocked and provoked by the all-pervading sense of evil and helplessness (one reviewer became so incensed and upset by the film that she even attempted to strike the director at the press showing); in Brazil authorities went to the extreme of banning it completely, regarding it as an incitement to terrorism and a threat to public order. Its ability to shock remains today.

The film's story, based on a Joseph Conrad novel, concerns a small-timer saboteur (Oscar Homolka), whose cover is as the owner of a cinema and who lives an outwardly normal, contented life with his wife (Sylvia Sydney) and her younger brother (Desmond Tester). After an initial attempt at disrupting London's electricity supply, which results in unintended hilarity for the city's population, Homolka's superiors force him to become more ruthless – and plant a bomb. The most controversial sequence occurs when the innocent Tester is asked to deliver a package to the heart of Leicester Square, unsuspecting that what he really carries is a bomb. The worst happens and the bomb

Sabotage, 1938

explodes – killing not only the boy but everyone on the packed bus on which he is travelling. 'I made a serious mistake in having the little boy die. The public was resentful,' Hitchcock said in later life. Indeed it was a memory which was to haunt him for the rest of his life.

There were a lot of personal touches from Hitchcock in the film. The greengrocer's shop was like the one his father had owned and he had grown up in; the small West End cinema was just like the one where he spent so many days of his youth, and Simpson's, where the detective has lunch, was in reality Hitchcock's own favourite restaurant. He had difficulties with his producer friend Ivor Montagu when he wanted to incorporate a real tram into the huge outdoor street set built for the film. Montagu complained it wasn't worth the cost, and emotions became so heated that after the completion of shooting the two men met only once again before Hitchcock's death in 1980. Hitchcock got his tram: a line was laid from the Lime Grove studios to a siding off White City. It cost £3,000 for the one day of shooting.

Sabotage is an astonishing cinematic *tour de force*, full of brilliant, terrifying scenes. It's also an uncannily melancholic piece, able to be one moment tense, the next desperately sad. One famous example of this is in the dinner scene, despite the initial problems caused by the leading lady. Sylvia Sydney had been brought over from Hollywood by co-producer Michael Balcon especially for the film, and was used to the American method of filming, whereby scenes would be shot in their entirety from different angles. She certainly wasn't prepared for Hitchcock's technique of shooting everything in little pieces and then putting it together like a jigsaw during editing. In the dinner scene she kills Homolka with a

Liam Redmond in *High Treason*, 1951

carving knife as they sit down to eat; but it became too much for her: half-hysterical, she broke down and ran crying from the set. It was only when she saw the final print that she realized what Hitchcock had been doing. Delighted and amazed, she stood up in the viewing theatre and exclaimed: 'Hollywood must hear of this!'

Some fifteen years later with *High Treason* (1951) the spy/saboteur was again examined by British film-makers, though this time (in the period following the War) it was no longer so easy to distinguish who was the enemy. With Homolka and his gloomy, haunted face, hollow eyes and clipped accent, we at least had definite suspicions: amongst the mounting paranoia of society in the early 1950s, even the most straightforward person could be revealed as a dangerous foreign agent. The movie's opening sequence establishes this idea perfectly, as we follow a timid office clerk going home at the end of the day. Once back in his flat he proceeds to feed the cat and then, quite matter-of-factly, he takes out hidden apparatus and begins to decode secret memos stolen from the Ministry of Defence: the result of his handiwork is shown in a sequence every bit as jolting as the explosion in *Sabotage*.

Again it starts innocently: the clerk meets a harmless-looking young man at a music society recital. He whispers the date that a munitions ship is arriving at London docks. Abruptly we are there on the appointed day – the bomb rips away half of the pier and leaves dead bodies scattered everywhere. The special-effects experts simulated the explosion by a complicated combination of animation and live-action footage, a process which took many weeks to perfect and edit together. For an audience watching it now, the result is still breathtaking.

The film was co-written and directed by Roy Boulting, and shot by Gilbert Taylor in a semi-documentary style, getting maximum use from the extensive location work. Indeed, *High Treason's* best scenes come when it leaves the studio. For the final, exciting sequence as the police battle against time and the saboteurs to try and stop another bomb being detonated, producer Paul Soskin managed to get permission to film inside Battersea Power Station itself (this was in the days when it was still an active source of electricity) and actors and crew – working around the shifts of the men there – were there for more than a week perfecting the fifteen-minute shoot-out. The authenticity of the drama on the screen was well worth it in the end.

The plot follows Commander Robert Brennan (Liam Redmond) and Superintendent Folland (André Morell) in their efforts to uncover the dangerous spy ring and the 'leak' in the Defence Department. The widespread appeal of the gang is shown when the investigation reveals a line of agents stretching from a dock foreman through various academics and finally to a respected MP, the leader of the so-called 'People's Peace Party'. The sensitive political position of Britain meant that controversy once again cast a shadow; the film was made in utmost secrecy, with guards posted to keep press and visitors away from the set, and the actual release of *High Treason* was delayed until the end of the year and after the

General Election of 1951. It was eight months old by the time the public saw it.

A year later, Anthony Asquith's *The Net* (1952) was a deliberately less down-to-earth and more melodramatic film featuring an East European spy whose mission is to try and steal a British secret invention, a super-fast aeroplane that in military terms could be of limitless power. Again the dilemma is proposed: whom do you trust – all of the personnel working on the M-7 project have been double-, even triple-checked and cleared by security. Nobody's honour is in doubt. Yet information is somehow getting out – a colleague and friend is a military spy. Psychologically, *The Net* is extremely plausible and convincing, revolving around the question of freedom, for the 'net' of the title refers to the prison-like manner in which the project's scientists are locked away from the outside world. The military and government authorities are mentally and physically suffocating them, one moment putting on the pressure to complete the project, the next saying it's a waste of time and money and threatening to shut the whole thing down. Thus what the craft's designer Heathley (James Donald) is offered by the spy, Dr Bord (Noel William), as the two of them crash through various speed barriers in the actual plane itself, is the opportunity to work however he pleases – if only he will defect to the East with his creation. There will be no demands to fulfil, no unknowledgeable superiors to be bossed by.

The film was a difficult one to make, since William Fairchild's script concentrated heavily on the study of characters under stress, and less on action/suspense set-pieces. Similarly, there were the problems of presenting an aircraft that looked (and sounded) believable as it breaks new scientific barriers that were not even known of in 1952. To overcome this, design experts worked for months on a shape and appearance that could be futuristic yet remain this side of sci-fi, whilst sound effects were borrowed from Farnborough research station. Another, more down-to-earth, problem occurred on the set one day towards the end of the shoot, when Donald's inflatable space-age suit developed a puncture. With valuable time being wasted, there was only one solution: before each take a production assistant was told to blow into it until it was reflated, and then block the hole with a cork.

By the 1960s British spy films were becoming not only uncertain about the hostile, foreign forces around them, but simultaneously disillusioned with the workings of Britain's own secret service. The Bond series were the flip-side to this, gadget-filled adventures for middle-aged kids; more typical of the developing trend was the downbeat *The Ipcress File* (1965), which introduced the character of Harry Palmer and made Michael Caine into an international star. The story was based on the bestselling Len Deighton novel, though the narrative twisted through so many confusing turns that it quickly became unimportant anyway. What mattered was the style and the mood. Director Sidney J. Furie has a penchant for unusual, clever angles, and the jagged editing and muted colour scheme served to accentuate this further. In an interview on location at

Michael Caine in *The Ipcress File*, 1965

Victoria railway station, Furie commented on the wet and dreary weather: 'Lovely day for filming. It will rain soon. Grey, gritty – that's the effect we are seeking. The film is being shot in colour but so monochrome you'd hardly notice. This is meant to be spying for real, whereas the Bond films are for glamorous pusses and jokes.'

The narrative strands that did remain intact involve Caine and his investigation into a "brain-drain" among scientists. His attempt to recover one particular missing professor, Radcliffe (Aubrey Richards), who has been kidnapped from a train after the murder of his bodyguard, leads on a trail of blackmail, assassination, coded tapes and brainwashing until it turns back on itself and unveils Caine's boss, Dalby (Nigel Green) as being crooked.

It all seems somewhat self-conscious and dated now, yet what keeps the interest of the viewer is the Caine/Palmer persona. It had been deliberately toned down from the original book to make him more 'ordinary': thus he wore glasses, had an overtly London accent, cooked his own food (though the ingredients always seemed ridiculously confused) and spent his day shopping at the nearby supermarket. In Deighton's conception, the character travelled in a helicopter and his case took him to Lebanon and a US missile base in the Pacific Ocean; by contrast Caine would only journey as far as the local bus could go. This incarnation of the 'common' spy proved so popular that it spawned two equally successful sequels, *Funeral in Berlin* (1966) and *Billion Dollar Brain* (1967).

One of the most memorable scenes from the film is the brainwashing that Caine has to battle his way through. It was played totally deadpan, with meticulous attention to quite vicious detail – there is tangible pain. *The Quiller Memorandum* (1966) similarly featured a devastating interrogation, this time with the evil Max Von Sydow persecuting the drugged George Segal. With its pessimistic vision of modern spy methods, however, it represented a complete change from the convoluted, breakneck plotting of *The Ipcress File*, since in Harold Pinter's sparse and studied adaptation of the Adam Hall pulp novel, *The Berlin Memorandum*, the story has been virtually dispensed with. Which was probably the point, an examination of a void in which events happen rather more by chance than design, where communication has broken down to the extent that simply nobody can talk without resorting to cryptic meanings. Trust certainly is a forgotten word. In a telling scene, Segal's superior, Alec Guinness, explains to him with the use of cutlery and food on a table how Segal is a lonely man caught in the middle between two opposing armies, both equally ruthless in disposing of him if he takes a wrong step – even his own side.

Producer Ivan Foxwell actually managed to get permission to film in Berlin, making it one of the first English-speaking pictures shot there. Reports at the time said that this was possible because, when presented with the script, the German authorities were unable to understand the story, though this was probably more publicist hype than anything else. What is for certain is the fact that the existence of neo-Nazi factions within Germany was a very

Alec Guinness in *The Quiller Memorandum*, 1966

Gabriel Byrne in *Defence of the Realm*, 1986

66

sensitive subject. Indeed, when the film was released there, a large part of it was censored: dialogue was cut from the soundtrack and dubbed over so as to blur any political bias; even the shirts were re-coloured on film from brown to red in order to shift the inference away from Nazism to communism.

It is worth noting that, until the time of *The Quiller Memorandum*, the spy film had faithfully preserved the cinematic conventions of always supplying a degree of romantic interest and seeking to conclude the story on an upbeat, reassuring note. Yet, as film-makers moved into the 1970s, the prevalent mood of unease and pessimism grew stronger and stronger until it dominated their work. Thus, whereas the saboteur is killed and the detective gets the girl of his dreams in *Sabotage*, in *Quiller*, Segal found that the 'girl' was in fact his enemy and there was seemingly nothing he could do.

A similar feeling pervades one of the best British thrillers in recent years, *Defence of the Realm* (1986). As with many modern films, it has not so much to do with 'typical spies', as they might have been previously labelled, as with people caught in a world where dangerous secrets are suppressed and where a pair of watching eyes seems to be round every corner. Except that in the 1980s, high-tech has superseded human facilities: when the unsuspecting hero clambers out of bed in the morning, there are now electronic cameras and microphones recording each movement and sound. The political ramifications of the plot bear similarities with *High Treason*, though here the problems have worsened. There are no clear-cut lines, no obvious factions seeking to uproot democracy – the threat is present already.

The story tells of a newspaper reporter, Nick Mullen (Gabriel Byrne), whose latest scoop involves an established MP and his mistress, suggested links with the KGB, and how this might be connected to the recent, mysterious death of a young man who escaped from prison in eastern England. What seemed a simple assignment begins to grow into something complicated and deadly, far beyond his control: the MP dies, a fellow journalist is murdered and Byrne finds his life under threat, fighting his way

through a jungle of deceit and cover-ups. The young director, David Drury, commented whilst shooting: 'It's not a tub-thumping film by any stretch of the imagination. What we've tried to do is get a happy balance between pure entertainment and something that is fairly pithy ... It's all conundrum essentially – a puzzle. The audience is put in the mind of the leading character, and he effectively takes us through the whole mystery.'

Denholm Elliott in *Defence of the Realm*, 1986

It was enthusiastically received by both audiences and critics, managing to garner a British Academy Award in the category of Best Supporting Actor for Denholm Elliot (in the role of an old-time, alcoholic journalist) and have a special presentation at the 1986 Cannes Film Festival in the Director's Fortnight selection. Both Drury and Byrne made their cinema débuts in the film, and it was perhaps their fresh talent (allowed scope after a background in television) that brought such verve and drama to the topics involved. For as well as taking a swipe at political hypocrisy, it took a look at the murky goings-on of tabloid newspapers. To do background research on this, Drury and Byrne visited the *Sunday Express* in Fleet Street and met the editor, Sir John Junor, so as to try and capture the atmosphere of the place and reproduce it. But owing to the critical light in which they intended to show a newspaper, they dared not present the real script – and decided instead to say that they were in the process of developing a new musical.

The greatest of all cinema spy stories is undoubtedly *The 39 Steps*, which has now been filmed some three different times: it is one of that rare breed of stories that is able to transcend the limitations of any given time period and appeal to audiences across five decades, oblivious of trends and fashions that might limit an inferior plot. The films are separated by roughly twenty years, and they obviously reflect radically different styles of film-making, yet what remains the single dominating factor linking them is a sense of fun and adventure that is wholly infectious. Not even the pressures and worries of our angst-ridden modern society can diminish that.

The curious paradox is that the original book by John Buchan was actually a rather stolid affair, and none of the films has really taken much notice of it other than as a basic outline. The most obvious example is with the title itself. In the book it refers to the number of steps leading down from the cliff-top to the landing place for the enemy spies, but the three films each have their own different theory: in the recent Robert Powell vehicle they were the number of steps leading up to the clock room in Big Ben; in the late-1950s Kenneth More version, they were steps at a certain point along the Thames; and in the first Robert Donat film, they more simply signified the name of the threatening foreign gang.

Of course it is the first version that remains, deservedly, the best known, for Hitchcock's 1935 movie was not just a landmark piece of British cinema in its own right, but also retains all the humour, excitement and surprises that it must have had on the première

Robert Donat in *The 39 Steps*, 1935

release. It was also a personal favourite of the director himself (even if he slept through its première at the New Gallery Theatre), something which is clearly shown by the fact that he virtually re-made it twice during his period in America: both *Saboteur* (1942) and *North By Northwest* (1959) pick up the same theme of a young man innocently on the run for a murder he did not commit, forced to chase after the real culprits in order to attempt to clear himself.

In fact, the narrative of *The 39 Steps* is patently ridiculous, and even by the end the audience is left with little inkling of what is going on. It starts with Richard Hannay (Donat) being approached by a mysterious woman (Lucy Mannheim) who tells him that she is a spy and begs for a place to stay for the night. Before dawn, however, she is dead, stumbling into Donat's bedroom, a knife firmly embedded in her back, mumbling the immortal and chilling words: 'Watch out Hannay ... they'll get you next!' From then on it's a madcap chase that takes Donat from London to Scotland and back again, until he proves his innocence in the music hall where the film began. Hitchcock manipulates our feelings of empathy towards the beleaguered Donat beautifully, playing on our emotional response to an ordinary man suddenly thrown into the confused and violent world of spies. Indeed it's a regular Hitchcock theme – that of the intrusion of a violent outside world upon the quiet, normal ways of everyday life.

Another typical Hitchcock motif – used for the first time in this film – was the blonde, ice-cool heroine. Later examples included Ingrid Bergman, Kim Novak, Grace Kelly and Eva-Marie Saint, but the initial personification was by Madeleine Carroll. Some of the most memorable scenes in the film occur when she is, much to her horror, handcuffed to Robert Donat. When shooting began on 11 January, 1935, the first takes were to be of the scenes where the couple escape from the enemy agents whilst still wearing the cuffs; it gave Hitchcock the perfect excuse to play one of his infamous (and cruel) practical jokes. As the two actors arrived on the set, he went rushing up to them and slapped the cuffs on, saying he wanted to let them get used to the feel before filming. What he did then was hide the key with the studio security guard, claim it was lost, and proceed to film insert shots of the sixty-two Scottish sheep which had been brought over from Hertfordshire for the day. His purpose was to embarrass the actors thoroughly, making sure they were stuck together for the whole day until he suddenly 'found' the key at around six o'clock. They didn't even shoot the handcuff scenes till the following morning.

The screen-writer of *The 39 Steps* Charles Bennett, said of Hitchcock: 'He was the biggest bully in the world; one of the kindest men I have ever met in my life.' In fact, Hitchcock's meddling later led on to common gossip on the set (whether it was true or not) that Carroll and Donat were having an affair. What is certain is that on the screen together the two stars are electric, as they progress from animosity, through friendship, to eventual love, the last scene ending as they tenderly hold hands.

Hitchcock was the director on his productions, right down to a despotic attitude he displayed in front of the crew and cast. The

Robert Donat and Madeleine Caroll in *The 39 Steps*, 1935

Kenneth More in *The 39 Steps*, 1960

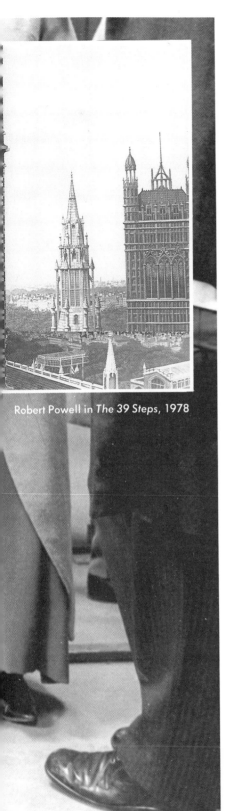
Robert Powell in *The 39 Steps*, 1978

start of each take was not signalled by calling 'action', but by throwing a piece of china and smashing it on the floor – on *The 39 Steps* he was at his tea-cup-throwing best.

The 1959 re-make, by utter contrast, was made by a British producer-director team who were anything but dictatorial in their approach to filmmaking. During the 1950s and 1960s, Betty Box and Ralph Thomas made some of the most successful home-based films, their output for Rank being roughly two a year; they were perhaps not the most critically acclaimed of partnerships, yet the product was always professional and reliable entertainment. One of the most impressive features of their work was their adaptability in terms of content, ranging from social drama to high comedy. It included *Appointment with Venus* (1951), *Campbell's Kingdom* (1957), *A Tale of Two Cities* (1958) and *No Love for Johnnie* (1961). Perhaps their most commercial venture was *Doctor in the House* (1954), and it was the re-teaming with its star, Kenneth More, that heralded the shooting of *The 39 Steps*. This fact is significant because their version was predominantly played for broad laughs, and as such (even though, scene for scene, it matches Hitchcock's version) probably explained why it lacked the suspense of the original. Still, it had compensations, especially in More and the co-star Tania Elg. It also extended the Hitchcockian theme of violence and mystery coming from the most unlikely places: Hannay (More) finds that in this film, even a nanny walking a baby-carriage through Hyde Park can turn out to be a spy.

By a macabre coincidence, on the day the 1978 *The 39 Steps* belatedly arrived for its first showing in New York, Alfred Hitchcock died. But he would have been proud of the latest version, directed by Don Sharp. Made on a budget of £950,000, it had a raw vitality that recalled the 1930s film. The writer, Michael Robson, cleverly relocated the story in the time of the novel, with England on the brink of the First World War, and thanks to some marvellously evocative camerawork by John Coquillon, it was an unusual and fresh setting. Robson stated before it opened: 'The date gave us wonderful currency with which to play, the collision of old and new worlds, as the hansom cab gives way to the car.' In fact, placing the story in 1914 posed a lot of problems as the art department scoured the country for authentic cars, furniture and even newspapers of the period. Similarly, the train adventures that supposedly take place on the journey to Scotland actually had finally to be relocated on the Severn Valley Railway, where the only available steam train could be found. In the end the film was part-Buchan, part-Hitchcock and part-new. It was all good fun though.

The best, and closing, sequence takes place as Hannay (Robert Powell) hangs from the minute hand atop Big Ben. It sums up the appeal of spy films, their ability to mix the incredible with the commonplace, the ability to take the audience into a new world yet one that is taking place in everyday life. They thrive on our willingness to believe the worst is happening. The problem is, it's probably true.

6

Fine and Dandy

For almost a decade, from the early 1940s through to the 1950s, a group of critically scorned films proved to be the box-office hits of their day. These were the costume pieces – high-flung, over-wrought melodramas. The ingredients were basic: passion, romance, sadism, heroism and plenty of sex; the characters were forceful: dominant women, devoted lovers and violent, cold-hearted husbands. They arrived on our screens at a time when Britain was in the midst of a desperate World War and the country longed for pure escapism.

The majority of British costume dramas were made by the productive and innovative Gainsborough Studios, located out in Islington, north London (they are collectively known as the 'Gainsborough Melodramas'). The company had been established in the late 1920s by Michael Balcon, and had been responsible for some of the most interesting films of the 1930s: the lavish musical *Chu Chin Chow*, the early Carol Reed efforts such as *Bank Holiday*, the Will Hay comedies, and Hitchcock's early British thrillers, *The Lady Vanishes* and *Young and Innocent*. However, it was upon the succession to administrative power of Edward Black and Maurice Ostrer that the change was made. Almost by accident, the rights to the novel *The Man in Grey* were acquired – and things were never to be the same again. The secret of their success was perhaps the family atmosphere which the small studio was able to foster and sustain. On each film it is the same key technicians behind the camera, and the same regular stars and supporting cast in front. Though it was not all by design: with the War on, personnel was necessarily at a minimum, with the result that everyone was pitching in to help, a position further accentuated by the relatively small budgets, and the fact that productions would invariably overlap.

Yet despite constraints of money and manpower, one of the most impressive features of these films is their lush veneer. They are uniformly stunning to watch, combining stark set design with stylish camerawork and opulent costumes to conjure up a distinctly sensual atmosphere, one that is deliberately unrealistic and overtly theatrical. (Indeed, the costume designer, Elizabeth Haffenden, graduated from West End shows.) Consequently the look is never historically accurate, retaining modern influences and touches so that the films seem to exist in some curious time warp. It lends them an ageless quality. Perhaps the nearest modern equivalent are the 'soaps' that flood our television screens – but even these are pale imitations. None of which is to claim that the films ought to be regarded as definitive cinematic masterpieces, simply that they should not be automatically dismissed, and that

Phyllis Calvert, Margaret Lockwood and James Mason in *The Man in Grey*, 1943

Margaret Lockwood and Phyllis Calvert in *The Man in Grey*, 1943

they deserve to be re-assessed as the wholly enjoyable entertainments their makers meant them to be.

Perhaps most of all, though, the Gainsborough melodramas are best remembered for the stars they created, a group of young talents which burst enthusiastically from the screen. The public was quick to respond: James Mason, the sexual, sadistic fiend women wanted to be hurt by; Stewart Granger, the dashing, well-mannered hero they wanted to be rescued by: Margaret Lockwood, the woman who knew what she wanted – and how to get it: Phyllis Calvert, the resilient innocent tempted and preyed upon by evil: and Patricia Roc, the bright epitome of the modern young woman.

Mason, Granger, Lockwood and Calvert were the four cornerstones of the films' continued appeal. Indeed, their first film together, *The Man in Grey* (1943), immediately catapulted them to stardom. In terms of style, it perhaps lacks the panache of the later productions: but the involved, twisting narrative and emotional conflicts (characters are motivated through escalating degrees of lust, jealousy and pride) more than compensate. During the actual shooting, director Leslie Arliss said in an interview: 'The background doesn't matter, it's the people you have in the foreground. I want to find a human story about real people. I am not afraid of sentiment and am working to overcome shyness and to put unashamed feelings on the screen rather than to depend on speed or action.' Little could he know, though, how phenomenally popular the results would be: audiences quickly helped it become the most financially successful film of the War.

The story involves the unhappy marriage of Clarissa (Phyllis Calvert) and Lord Rohan (James Mason), both of whom are in love with other people: Calvert with an actor, Rokeby (Stewart Granger)

and Mason with the cunning, vengeful Hesther (Margaret Lockwood). When Calvert decides that loyalty to the state of marriage supersedes her own feelings and refuses to elope with Granger, it all builds to a shattering climax, as Calvert is murdered by Lockwood who is then, in turn, thrashed to death by Mason.

It was only by accident that the film was ever made. At the time cinemas were still packed with the heroics of British and American war movies, and only the determined, astute Maurice Ostrer believed he had a potentially hot property with Lady Eleanor Smith's novel. It was eventually made at the disused factory that had been transformed into Gainsborough's two sound stages out at Islington, on a budget of £95,000 – one-third less than the average English production in 1943. It was released in August of that year – and by the beginning of 1944 fan magazines were unanimous in bestowing on it Best Film awards.

Public reaction was particularly strong for Mason and Lockwood, although neither had originally intended to be in it: Margaret Lockwood said she was simply unprepared for such a nasty character, but had finally realized it was too good a part to miss; whilst James Mason had been first cast in Granger's role, with Eric Portman set to portray Rohan, 'the man in grey'. The greatest uproar caused by the film came from the final confrontation scene, when Mason sadistically kills Lockwood with a whip. It created a whirlpool of outraged/excited letters from female fans convinced that Mason was like that in real life: 'Are you really like that?', 'Do you treat your wife in the same way?' In the end the actor struck back and wrote a short article for the magazine *Lilliput* entitled 'YES, I beat my wife'. The whipping sequence is pure Gainsborough: beautiful people pictured in a glorious Regency setting, where emotions are liable to (and do) explode into sexual violence at any moment.

Following on chronologically in the Gainsborough series, *Fanny by Gaslight* (1944) proved that *The Man in Grey* had been no flash in the pan. Again there were packed audiences wherever the film was shown, and this time even the critics responded warmly. Director Anthony Asquith certainly had toned down the over-heated emotions and introduced a more realistic atmosphere, but it is still the more melodramatic moments which stick in the mind, with James Mason once again the dark, brooding villain – one moment suave and charming, the next malicious and cruel. In an archetypal Gainsborough scene he is out in a restaurant with his wife, played by Margaretta Scott: continually he gazes around at the surrounding tables, smiling at any attractive women until, exasperated, Scott demands attention and a confirmation of his love. Mason simply turns to her and quietly states, as he kisses her hand: 'I've never loved you.'

James Mason in *The Man in Grey*, 1943

Mason's character is a vital part of the melodramas (a mantle mainly inherited by Dennis Price in later films), seemingly without any sort of motivation to inspire the unrelieved depravity and cruelty in which he indulges but nevertheless proving a powerful and charismatic figure. Mason himself was unable to explain fully how he played the parts. On *The Man in Grey* he said it was due to his inability to get on with director Arliss. 'I wallowed in a stupidly black mood throughout and since my own imagination had contributed nothing to the character who appeared on the screen, I have to conclude that only my permanent aggravation gave the character colour and made it some sort of memorable thing'. Indeed, the fact that he seemed to be able to play these parts with such ease always disturbed Mason, who felt it was revealing a subdued aspect of his own personality; perhaps the reason for his popularity was that he also awakened the dark side of the viewer.

Phyllis Calvert, in the title role of Fanny, also gives a fine performance, and an extremely demanding one, as she has to register developing emotions and a growing sense of responsibility. Based on the bestselling Michael Sadlier novel, the story centres round her tempestuous life, from an initially happy childhood home to the degredation of poverty and servitude, before her eventual salvation in the form of true love (and Stewart Granger, naturally).

The budget was once again a relatively low one (£90,000), but Asquith and cameraman Arthur Crabtree use the cramped interiors

James Mason and Margaret Lockwood in
The Wicked Lady, 1945

to great effect. This was mainly achieved by the clever placing of mirrors to give the appearance of depth and size that the sets would not otherwise have. The public loved every second – the film grossed more than £300,000 on the first release and guaranteed the continuation of Gainsborough Studios for the next decade.

With the third film, Gainsborough began to perfect the formula, melding the visual elements of *Fanny by Gaslight* with the helterskelter histrionics of the *Man in Grey* to create a deliciously absurd whole. Once again the source material was a well-known novel, though little but the premiss remained intact. *Madonna of the Seven Moons* (1944) is shot through with burning passion and longing which burn from every frame, and is unmitigated melodrama from start to finish.

The central casting re-teams Phyllis Calvert and Stewart Granger, the former giving another impressive performance as the schizophrenic Madalena/Rosanna (see chapter 3), outwardly the quiet, discreet wife of an Italian wine merchant, yet bottling up hidden desires and rages which periodically take over. She literally becomes a different person – the gypsy lover to Granger's small-time Florentine robber, Nino. Thanks to Calvert's skilful acting, they never become separate identities, for she imbues each with vestiges of the other, such that the dual-personality ploy is always convincing. For the actress it was a welcome break from the virginal innocents with which she was becoming identified. Indeed, for that reason producer R.J. Minney hadn't primarily considered her for the part. But her ability to transform from wildness to conformity within the turn of a head eventually won them over.

One of the most interesting aspects of *Madonna of the Seven Moons* is the picture of woman that the film unveils. As Calvert lies dead at the end, her husband (John Stuart) and lover (Granger) place, respectively, a cross and a rose on her breast: this symbolic picture of her torn personality was an especially pertinent one to the female audience in war-torn Britain, where the old ideals of morality and 'the womans place' were at last being questioned. In the film the conflict is finally resolved in the person of Angela (Patricia Roc), who sums up a new attitude – a liberal-minded, independent young woman showing a form of emancipation and freedom that society in general was just beginning to deal with.

The publicity sold the film on its romance and especially 'the searing love scenes'. In one of these, the Gainsborough style is shown to the full. Censorship at the time prevented showing a couple on a bed without each having at least one foot on the floor; to overcome this, the scene was shot in darkness, with Calvert and Granger seen in silhouette, their intense faces briefly illuminated only when Granger takes a drag on his cigarette. It is beautiful to watch, overtly suggestive and very powerful. In a review of the time, the *Manchester Guardian* said: 'Arthur Crabtree has directed this superior thriller as if it were a work of art,' and it is the imagination and flair of Crabtree, Italian designer Andrew Mazzei and cameraman Jack Cox that elevate the film beyond the boundaries of melodrama.

James Mason in *Fanny by Gaslight*,
1943

Many regard *The Wicked Lady* (1945) as the epitome of the Gainsborough melodramas. Undoubtedly it is one of the most gloriously over-the-top, as Margaret Lockwood, bored aristocratic housewife by day, takes to the country roads by night as a fearless highwaywoman, robbing coaches and seducing any man she thinks attractive. And Lockwood is perfect. Again she at first refused the part – but in the end it was, as she called it, 'too meaty' to refuse. Director Leslie Arliss said in a magazine article, 'she represents an elemental character, full of the most human and natural passions and forced by her own desires into crimes the result of which she can never escape'. Despite the virtual unanimity of the critics in hating every single moment, the public flocked to see it and made it the biggest money-maker of the year.

The novel on which the film was based, *The Life and Death of the Wicked Lady Skelton*, was actually suggested to Arliss by Lady Eleanor Smith, who had written the book from which the earlier film *The Man in Grey* was taken. The moment he started to read it, he knew he had the perfect material from which to make the next film. Immediately he rushed to Maurice Ostrer, the head of Gainsborough, and pleaded with him to buy the adaptation rights. Smiling, Ostrer informed the surprised Arliss that it was too late – he had already bought them just a fortnight before, with the intention that Arliss would direct.

Arliss received another more serious surprise upon the film's completion: the Hayes Office (the censor of films in America) refused to allow *The Wicked Lady* to be shown in the US. Apparently the dresses worn by Margaret Lockwood and Patricia Roc were too low-cut and revealed far too much of their bosom. Since the US market was so large and of such commercial importance, there was only one option left – the scenes that the Americans found 'offensive' would have to be re-shot. It may seem ridiculous to the modern viewer, but that is exactly what happened. The technical difficulties were enormous, with costumes and sets, long since scrapped, having to be painstakingly reconstructed exactly as they had been before. Yet there was no other choice – more than twelve months after they had originally finished shooting all the cast and crew had to be reassembled to make a less rude duplicate version.

Today the film remains enjoyable nonsense (certainly far superior to the recent re-make) that is never less than entertaining. Yet for all its reputation, it somehow ultimately remains a stagy piece. Leslie Arliss has not an instinctively cinematic eye, and so despite Jack Cox's sumptuous lighting and John Bryan's fascinatingly detailed sets, it becomes unfortunately stodgy.

In *Caravan* (1946), however the elements all gel stunningly together. The director was the former cameraman Arthur Crabtree, and he brought to the film a supreme visual sheen. His two previous directorial attempts had been *Madonna of the Seven Moons* and another Gainsborough picture, *They Were Sisters* (1944), but neither possesses the sheer verve and confidence that he displays here. He was aided by a slightly higher budget than usual, and John Bryan was able to use the full scope of the sound stages to construct some towering and near-abstract sets: they were the biggest ever built for a Gainsborough production, and were mounted on huge sliding rollers so that they could be pushed aside or folded away on the spot, enabling the camera to swoop and dive through seemingly impossible movements. The photography by Stephen Dade is another plus, continually on the prowl through richly and dramatically lit streets and rooms, milking every ounce of atmosphere from each shot; and the editor, Charles Knott, cuts at such a breathtaking pace that even though the film is remarkably long for its type (longer than two hours), it never grows boring. But it is Crabtree's flamboyance that dominates, taking the viewer into the realm of another, almost surrealistic world. The pity was that in later years his undoubted talent was never fully utilized, and though he made some moderately successful films (and even the notorious horror piece *Horrors of the Black Museum* (1959), which was widely criticized for its explicit violence), the list is not impressive. *Caravan* remains a testament to what could have been.

The story of *Caravan* is as melodramatic and incomprehensible as you could hope for. At the centre is the recurring conflict of flaming, uncontrollable passion and mannered, restrained civility, the opposing poles of the argument this time personified by two younger members of the Gainsborough repertory (both of them having served their apprenticeship in minor parts in previous films): the rumbustious, sexy Jean Kent and the demure, pretty

James Mason in *Fanny by Gaslight*, 1943

81

Anne Crawford. And of course, smiling and swaggering his way through the proceedings is the inimitable Stewart Granger. He plays Richerd Darell, aspiring writer, who finds himself split from his fiancée Oriana (Crawford) when he is asked to take some valuable jewellery to Spain by the wealthy Don Carlos, who in turn has promised to publish his first novel. But arch-rival Francis (Dennis Price), determined to win Crawford's hand, dispatches his servant to make sure that Granger never returns. As a result Granger is attacked and robbed and left for dead. Gypsy dancer Rosa (Jean Kent) saves him, however, and nurses Granger back to health. She also introduces (and seduces) him to the uninhibited gypsy way of life.

It is eventually resolved in a welter of violence and emotion that ignites from the cooker-pot atmosphere of sweltering sexuality. One of the most interesting aspects of this carefully sustained atmosphere is the intelligent use of sound. Walter Hyden's music was specially composed to interact with the action when it built to a crescendo: in this way the sound of a gunshot or of a punch in a fight coincides with the crashing noise of loud percussion, highlighting its impact and making it that more dramatic. Another example is with Elizabeth Haffenden's plush costume design: into Jean Kent's flowing gypsy gowns small bells were subtly sewn, so that when she danced there was this continuous, delicate tinkling sound.

Kent's erotically choreographed dances exemplify the powerful use of music in these melodramas. A vital part of the Gainsborough formula is to link the romantic elements with a strong, easily memorable theme that weaves its way in and out of the film. In *The Wicked Lady* it was Patricia Roc's love song; in *Madonna of the Seven Moons*, Phyllis Calvert's sad signature tune. With *The Magic Bow* (1946), though, the music actually took over and became like another character. The film purported to tell the story of the violinist Niccolò Paganini and his rise to fame as the greatest musician of his time, but its concentration was shifted more to his romantic life, and most especially the difficulties with his true love, Jeanne de Vermond. In itself, it is a rather frivolous and slow-moving movie, despite the careful work of the technicians (especially of the designers, Andrew Mazzei and John Bryan, in their re-creation of Genoa), and in comparison to the other films it is certainly disappointing; but there is still much to enjoy.

Particularly strong is the casting of Stewart Granger, whose impersonation of the moody, short-tempered but wholly charismatic Italian is quite captivating. Originally the part had been assigned to James Mason, who had spent weeks practising with a violin so as to get his miming to the music perfect. In the end he fell out because of creative differences with director Bernard Knowles, and subsequently sent his violin to Granger's dressing room with condolences for the work he'd have to do with the instrument. Granger picked up the challenge with enthusiasm though, and his playing is extremely convincing: face furrowed with determined intensity, his fingers fly across the strings with the confidence of someone who has been playing all his life.

Stewart Granger in *The Magic Bow*,
1946

Opposite Granger in *The Magic Bow* is Phyllis Calvert – a teaming which marked their fourth and last time on screen together. She looks perhaps at her most attractive in this film, exuding charm and emotion through every scene, and most especially in the final reconciliation sequence, where, shimmering in a rippling, sequinned white dress, she fulfils the conception of the romantic heroine. In reality the two stars didn't get on very well, but on celluloid none of this animosity is reflected: as screen lovers they both radiate a charm and passion that is wholly endearing.

The Magic Bow proved to be the last production initiated by the Ostrer and Black management, and was intended to be a prestige piece. As such it was even given its world première at the Cannes Film Festival. Its best claim to fame was the hiring of Yehudi Menuhin to play the violin solos. Producer R.J. Minney flew him from America, with Stradivarius and player himself both expensively insured at Lloyds of London. It was worth it. The playing is not merely some elaborate publicity stunt: it adds

Jean Kent in *Caravan*, 1946

another dimension, and when mixed with the visuals of Granger provides the viewer with a serene and touching brand of film magic.

Sydney Box became the new boss of Gainsborough Studios in 1947, after the enormous commercial success of his famous James Mason and Anne Todd melodrama, *The Seventh Veil* (1946). At the time this film was one of few which had ever been so popular (it played to full houses in one New York theatre for more than six months), and though Gainsborough films were still raking in hefty profits, it was felt that his dynamism and experience could only be of benefit. During his tenure, the company made its last two costume melodramas. (Box and his wife shifted the emphasis towards modern melodramas, concentrating on contemporary, controversial problems.) The first of these was the lavish *Jassy* (1947). In a recent interview, designer John Bryan revealed how he was told that 'this was the big one – we could do anything', and from a technical basis it is quite magnificent. Jack Asher's beautiful Technicolor photography creates a dream-like atmosphere, whilst Elizabeth Haffenden, who did months of film tests to adapt from the black-and-white designs she had been used to on her past projects, provided some sublime dresses, a wondrous combination of soft pastel shades. And the sets (on which 90 percent of the film was shot) are quite outstanding in their scope and texture – powerful reminders of a bygone era of film-making.

Director Bernard Knowles was too concerned with these outward trimmings, though, and not wary enough of the uncertain narrative. It begins promisingly with drunkenness, suicide and a gypsy girl with powers to see into the future. The girl is Jassy Woodruffe (Margaret Lockwood), and it is her story that is mainly followed, through the murder of her father, her friendship with Dilys (Patricia Roc), the revenge on the man who killed her father, and her eventual happiness in the arms of Barney (Dermot Walsh), a friend from childhood. Yet Lockwood's character changes so rapidly – from revenge to forgiveness – that the viewer is left with no story thread to hang on to; others are equally ill defined and undeveloped. Reports of difficulties and delays in shooting account for some of this, but cannot excuse it all.

Jassy's best moments come when it resorts to Gainsborough's old style of visual dream: the lord (Basil Sydney) exploding into sadistic violence when he sees his wife being unfaithful; the villager beating his young daughter senseless in the kitchen: or Roc suddenly saved from the savage force of her father by being whisked away to an awaiting carriage in the arms of her young beau. The violence, in fact, gained a deal of notoriety at the time, critics branding Box a cheap sensationalist: one reviewer wrote: 'some film-makers like to put their own personal signature on each film that they make ... Alfred Hitchcock, for example, always makes an appearance on the screen. But Sydney Box likes to distinguish himself by a gratuitous surplus of sadism'. It forced the producer to defend his artistic principles in an open letter to the press, in which he complained that he was simply trying to produce a piece of honest entertainment.

Filming *The Magic Bow*, 1946

Yehudi Menuhin playing a violin solo for *The Magic Bow*, 1946

Box courted trouble of quite another kind with *The Bad Lord Byron* (1948), which caused a stir both in England and America before a single foot of film had even been shot. The first problem was over the title itself, which caused a flood of angry letters to arrive on Sydney Box's doorstep saying he was degrading one of the country's finest poets – before the script had been finished. The press inflamed matters, managing to condemn the film and almost cause production to stop. Meanwhile in the US there were censorship problems. Not because of the content of the screenplay that was presented to the censors, but because of the subject-matter itself. They simply regarded the fact that a biography was being planned on such an outrageous character as reprehensible. Attacked from every side, Box decided he would prove them all wrong and make a film that was entertaining, truthful and tasteful.

above left, Margaret Lockwood and Patricia Roc in *Jassy*, 1947
above, Patricia Roc in *Jassy*, 1947
below left, Dennis Price in *Bad Lord Byron*, 1948

Without doubt the lengths he went to to provide historical accuracy were extraordinary. For example, actual Byron furniture appears in some scenes (in the ones showing Byron in his London club you can see the poet's own dining table and chairs), and when such items could not be used they were scrupulously copied and built. The same was true for the costumes, which were reproduced down to the very stitching. In fact, the struggle to finish in time for shooting was so great that the studio had to get help in: only the best were employed though, in this case from the Ministry of Labour's embroiderers, whose other assignment at the time was making Princess Elizabeth's wedding dress. Even Byron's shoes were minutely studied so that Dennis Price (who was playing the part) could get the character's famous limp exactly right. The problem was that it became such a habit for Price that he would continue to limp even after he had finished the take and walked off the set.

In terms of costume melodrama, the blend came nearer to being right with *The Bad Lord Byron*. Historical truth was there, but the framework of the story and the nature of the romantic element was close to the original Gainsborough method. The narrative begins at Byron's deathbed in Greece, and then goes to a heavenly court where a judge presides over the 'case' as to whether Byron was either 'good' or 'bad'. The women in his life dominate the story, and again come to signify the different social attitudes of society: Sonia Holm the quiet, sensible woman; Mai Zetterling the passionate Italian lover; and Joan Greenwood the pathetic figure torn between the two – an apt reflection for British women at the time who, with the War over, were finding their new-found independence quashed, as the returning males expected them to return to their old positions of inferiority. The director, David McDonald, aided by Stephen Dade's shiny photography, stirs it all around with consummate style. The film comes to represent the end of an era in film-making – the end of the Gainsborough costume melodrama; *The Bad Lord Byron*, though not a success in its day, has improved with age and now appears a swansong to be proud of.

There were other companies willing to continue the genre (after all, the films could still be pretty reliable moneymakers), but somehow nobody else was able to reproduce the necessary kind of approach. *Blanche Fury* (1948) was a good try, which wisely recruited Stewart Granger as the male lead and brought in the old Gainsborough designer John Bryan to co-ordinate the startling sets. The production company was Cineguild, and the film boasted some lovely colour photography and a storyline ripe with burgeoning emotion: young Blanche (Valerie Hobson) determines to make an independent, easy life for herself with distant relatives, the Furys; but her cold façade crumbles when she falls in love with Philip Thorn (Granger) who has sworn to destroy the entire Fury family for robbing him of his inheritance, and she finds herself trapped in plans of murder and intrigue. The producer was Anthony Havelock-Allen, the man responsible for the conception of *In Which We Serve* (1942), and the respected producer of *This Happy Breed* (1945) and *Brief Encounter* (1946). The director was a Frenchman, Marc Allégret, best known for his work on Alexander Korda's *The Thief of Baghdad* (1940). They brought a cool, classical touch to the film, but one which lacked the wild, passionate sense of atmosphere that was the secret of Gainsborough.

A similar fault marred *Hungry Hill* (1949), a Two Cities production. The notable writing credits list the novelist Daphne du Maurier (it was one of her few screenplays) and Terrence Fisher (who later became famous for his spirited direction of the early Hammer horrors), and indeed the script was surprisingly literate. Unfortunately, the story moves in fits and starts as it covers the forty-year feud between two ancient Irish families over the possession of the hill of the title. The best scenes come when the large budget is fully utilized – such as in the burning of the town or the huge dance sequence – and there are some good performances, especially the playful Margaret Lockwood, the mellow Dennis Price and the agonized Cecil Parker. The attention to detail is formidable: the art director, Vetchinsky, spent months gathering together facts, old maps, plans and photos so that his construction of the copper mine would be exact to the last plank of wood; Eleanor Abbey, the costume designer, studied for weeks at the British Museum in order that the clothes would be perfect; even musicians were hand-picked and carefully trained to play instruments of the period.

But there was no real life left in these films any more. When the talented director Joseph Losey tried to resuscitate further the genre ten years later with *The Gypsy and the Gentleman* (1957), Rank got poor returns from the £250,000 they had invested. It was another splendid-looking film, but it came across emotionally limp. (In a Losey retrospective held in Paris during the 1960s, the director requested that the film be shown silently, since he felt the images were tableaux that managed to tell their own story.) The film's success was intended to revolve about the tempestuous, passionate Melina Mercouri – but the timing was wrong and she came across as merely frantic. As befitted the size of the budget, there were things to enjoy, but it mainly proved that in the gritty, downbeat 1950s the exuberant costume melodramas had no place.

right, Margaret Lockwood in *The Wicked Lady*, 1945

far right, Dennis Price and Joan Greenwood in *Bad Lord Byron*, 1948

right, Stewart Granger and Valerie Dobson in *Blanche Fury*, 1948

above right, *Hungry Hill*, 1946

above and left, Margaret Lockwood

British films had moved on and somehow lost the frenetic, wild and erotic feel that the Gainsborough lady represented. She and her productions, though, remain with us to entertain for many

7
The War Game

Lili Palmer in *Conspiracy of Hearts*, 1960

Over decades of film-making on the subject of war, the 'image' of the serviceman and civilian have gone through many a transition. In the late 1930s and early 1940s we saw portrayed on the screen the clean-cut hero, the fearless patriot, the resourceful resistance fighter and the prisoner of war obsessed with escape. On the other side of the coin, we saw the unsympathetic pacifist, the shell-shocked victim, the despicable coward and – the most heinous of all – the traitor.

On the Home Front, war films became even more poignant as ordinary people endured shortages of food, were made homeless by air attacks, suffered the heartbreak of losing their loved ones, and lived round the clock with the constant threat of imminent enemy invasion. All these adversities were shown being faced with stiff-upper-lip resolution, unswerving loyalty to our leaders and the cause, and a cheerful disposition that traversed all class barriers. Dozens of films attempted to represent the stoical British citizen in the back-to-the-wall situation. The tireless men and women of the Ambulance Corps, the Air Raid Wardens, the Voluntary Fire Service, the munitions workers, the Home Guard – all going about their duties with gritty determination. Again, they had their vilified counterparts. The conscientious objectors, the black marketeers, the spivs and the enemy within, the Fifth Columnist.

But these black-and-white definitions, often creating stereotypes, were slowly to change. War dramas began to become more complex as they distanced themselves from events and the strictures of government-inspired propaganda. Psychiatry and psychology had become, albeit briefly, box-office, and war films started to incorporate into their storylines attitudes of self-examination.

In the late 1950s and early 1960s, British films began to question the morality of war, and took, if somewhat uneasily at first, the standpoint of formerly hated adversaries. The Italians, in a whitewashing exercise, were now being represented as warm-hearted people who in reality, it transpired, had detested Mussolini and all that he stood for. In *Conspiracy of Hearts* (1960), this is demonstrated admirably when a Mother Superior, played by Lily Palmer, is condemned to death by a German Army officer for her part in rescuing Jewish children from a concentration camp, and she faces a firing squad of Italian soldiers. To a man, the Italians fire the first salvo over the Mother Superior's head and the second one straight at the German officer. This was in sharp contrast to earlier films such as *The Malta Story* (1953), where there were graphic scenes of the Italian air force bombing the Maltese population during day and night air raids.

The Malta Story, 1953

Jack Hawkins, Alec Guinness and
Anthony Steele in *The Malta Story*, 1953

A Town Like Alice, 1956

After many films had shown us how we had all inexplicably misunderstood the Italians' active part against us during the Second World War, the film-makers then turned their attention to the Japanese, and it seemed that we had misunderstood their role in the War as well. It is difficult to comprehend now, after watching the brutalities of the Japanese soldiers against defenceless women prisoners, as depicted with almost documentary realism in *A Town Like Alice* (1956), that we could ever be expected to extend our sympathies to that race again, and yet that is exactly what we did when films were made showing the aftermath of Hiroshima and Nagasaki.

Although war films have always had a popular appeal at the box office, especially such First World War classics as *Journey's End* (1930) and *All Quiet on the Western Front* (1930), which covered events leading up to the action and the slaughter that followed; it was just before, and during, the Second World War that the war film really came of age. This can partly be attributed to the sense of realism brought to the screen by the documentary school of film-makers, men like Alberto Cavalcanti, and, later, Harry Watt, who joined Ealing Studios from the ranks of the Crown Film Unit. The Ministry of Information, which was effectively the driving force of the British propaganda campaign, had watched at first with stunned admiration the effect of Goebbels's propaganda efforts in Germany.

The influences he had brought to bear on the media – in particular film, both dramatic and documentary, had stirred and aroused the German people into believing not only that they were the master race, but that they were invincible.

The Ministry of Information moved into action in a much more subtle way than Goebbels. Not for them the mass hysteria of the Nuremberg rallies, and the ranting and raving of Hitler, or the cream of Aryan youth displaying gymnastic skills and marching in goose-stepping time to brass bands, banners waving. They showed, through the Crown Film Unit documentaries and newsreel outlets such as Pathé, Movietone and Gaumont British, that not only could the British 'take it', they were also girding their loins to 'give it'. And it was this message that was passed on loud and clear to our film-makers, a message that was to become their creative motivation. That they took up the gauntlet, accepted the challenge and coped with it splendidly, is now a matter of history.

In 1940 the Minister of Information, Sir A. Duff Cooper, had placed Kenneth Clark in charge of the newly established Films Division of the MoI. Clark approached Michael Powell and asked him if he'd be interested in making an officially sponsored feature film. He told Powell that he would give him *carte blanche* on the subject of minesweeping. But Powell rejected that idea. He did tell Clark, however, that he would be interested in making a film in Canada. He went on to explain that he had been reading an article in a Sunday newspaper that made it obvious to him that, with Canada being right next door to the United States, any involvement Canada had with us in the War might stir the Americans' conscience and bring them into the conflict too. Clark agreed with Powell's reasoning, and thought it a good enough idea to ask the Government for a small grant of about £4,000 for Powell to go to Canada and get official co-operation in the making of this film.

As a result of Powell's visit in 1941, a most impressive combination of talent was assembled. It was financed by Rank and the MoI, who drew funds from a Treasury grant to make propaganda feature films. The film, written, produced and directed by Michael Powell and Emeric Pressburger, was called *49th Parallel* and had quite a high budget for that time. Powell and Pressburger worked on a small percentage of the profits in lieu of fees. But Powell claimed the film grossed £2 million. In today's terms, this would be the equivalent of a Stephen Spielberg or George Lucas blockbuster.

49th Parallel featured, in cameo roles, Leslie Howard, Laurence Olivier, Eric Portman, Raymond Massey and Anton Walbrook. Its storyline deals with six survivors of a German submarine crew after their U-boat is sunk in the Gulf of St Lawrence by the Royal Canadian Air Force. In a series of overlapping episodes, the survivors' numbers are gradually reduced as they are variously confronted by the changes in their circumstances. At the beginning of their journey across Eastern Canada, the Nazis take refuge in a Hutterite settlement of expatriate Germans. Their leader (Anton Walbrook) gives a powerful and moving speech, in which he utterly condemns the doctrine of Nazism and rejects out of hand

Jack Hawkins in *The Malta Story*, 1953

the idea that all Germans are brothers, expounding instead the virtues of living in a free country like Canada.

Eric Portman in The 49th Parallel, 1941

When at last only two active survivors are left, they come into conflict with Philip Armstrong-Scott (Leslie Howard), an English egg-head and expert on Indian culture. After he has extended them his hospitality, the Nazis taunt and goad him about his 'soft' way of life until they push him too far, and turn the gentle pacifist into a man seeking, and finding, revenge (see chapter 1). The final Nazi survivor, Lieutenant Hirth (Eric Portman), is cornered by a Canadian solider (Raymond Massey) who is temporarily absent without leave, on a train bound for the undefended 49th Parallel, situated between Canada and the (then neutral) USA. On reaching the border of the two countries, Lieutenant Hirth pleads with the US Customs officers to give him political assylum. But they turn a deaf ear, and send the train shunting back into Canada, showing the world exactly where their sympathies lie.

The sitting-on-the-fence policy of the US, although carefully understated in the script, was not lost on its audiences, and the film proved a very effective attempt to show the dangers of the Nazi mentality, and contrast this with our own democratic philosophy. The fanatics versus the lovers of freedom – the point was made in a most profound manner.

A review in the *Documentary News Letter* stated that *49th Parallel* was one of the best-made films ever produced in this country. The national press went on to rave about Leslie Howard's performance, and Eric Portman moved into the 'star' category as a result of his portrayal of the Nazi Lieutenant Hirth.

Perhaps an even more important film in the attempt to bolster up British morale was *In Which We Serve* (1941). It remains as one of the best examples of the genre, and will always be identified with that great original, Noel Coward. He dedicated the film to his friend, a naval officer whom he very much admired, Lord Louis Mountbatten, and to the crew of HMS *Kelly*. The *Kelly* had been sunk in similar circumstances to those of the ship in the film, HMS *Torrin*, and Mountbatten often attended the filming in the studio to give Coward advice and encouragement.

The message of *In Which We Serve* concerned itself with comradeship and a sense of national pride which was shared by the whole country, whether on the Home Front or in the Armed Forces. The theme of Britain fighting as one in the common cause was the main thrust of the story. It showed how the captain, officers and men of a destroyer behaved as 'a happy efficient unit' in peace time and at war. After their ship has been sunk at the Battle of Crete, we are taken through a series of individual flashbacks as they hang on to a Carley float with only their indomitable spirit keeping them alive. Noel Coward played Captain 'D' with an almost tongue-in-

Noel Coward in *In Which we Serve*, 1942

cheek understatement, expressing middle-class attitudes, which, although not always understood by Americans, nor for that matter by the British working classes, always commanded respect, representing as they did the sturdy backbone of Britain. At the other end of the social scale, the ratings were shown to be tough, loyal, resilient, witty and possessing all the other essential characteristics that would qualify them as 'the salt of the earth'.

Apart from the almost overwhelming presence of Noel Coward, the cast included many virtually unknown actors, who went on to become major screen stars, notably Richard Attenborough, John Mills, and the superb Celia Johnson. The film also gave the now acclaimed David Lean his first opportunity to direct some of the scenes. He worked on the film as Coward's associate, after spending more than ten years of obscurity in the cutting room as a film editor. In Which We Serve had the most enormously favourable propaganda impact, and was chosen by the United States National Board of Review of Motion Pictures as 'the outstanding film of 1942'.

Coward's memorable speech when addressing his crew may today seem almost laughable in view of what we now know was to come, but when he said: 'then we'll send Hitler a telegram saying "the Torrin's ready, you can start your war" ...' it struck exactly the right note, corresponding as it did with the mood of the nation at the time.

But for all the stiff-upper-lipness of the film, it did have its lighter moments off-screen. John Mills in his autobiography tells the story of how the character he was playing – that of Able Seaman Shorty Blake – was required, after the sinking of the Torrin, to swim in the studio tank, which had been suitably doctored with diesel oil and other gungey substances and débris, and make his way to one of the Carley floats. In the process he was supposed to be shot in the arm by a machine-gun bullet from an enemy plane which was strafing the survivors of the crew. This caused the special-effects man endless problems; no matter what he did, he just could not make the scene realistic enough. At last he had a brainwave. A runner was sent to the nearest chemist's shop, and he returned hastily, if somewhat embarrassed, with dozens of packets of male contraceptives. These were then fastened, at intervals of a foot, to a long length of tubing, which was drilled with holes corresponding to points where the contraceptives had been attached. The apparatus was then wired electrically and carefully lowered into the tank. On the command 'action' Mills himself was dropped into the murky water and struck out towards the float. At the appropriate moment, there was a rapid series of staccato explosions. They had blown compressed air into the tube and sent an electric charge down the wire. Mills felt a sharp crack in his right arm, shouted in pain, and was promptly heaved aboard the float. He claims, and there is little chance that he will ever be challenged, that he is the only actor who has been 'shot' in the arm by a 'French letter'.

A much more unusual and, as it turned out, controversial war film was made in 1943, produced by that prolific team, Powell and

Noel Coward and John Mills in *In Which We Serve*, 1942

Pressburger. *The Life and Death of Colonel Blimp* starred Anton Walbrook, Deborah Kerr and Roger Livesey. It was Powell and Pressburger's first film for their new company, and was very loosely based on the character created by the British cartoonist, David Low. Blimp, as depicted by Low, was a member of the upper class, the personification of those who thought that the British Empire was a nation on which the sun would never set. His views were right wing in the extreme – he was, in fact, the British equivalent of the diehards who had helped Hitler's rise to power in Germany.

It had been Powell's original conception to have Blimp played as a man reflecting extreme bigotry – a sort of aristocratic Alf Garnett – but without the humour. Powell's Blimp would have been 'vicious, slashing, cruel and merciless'. The MoI, however, were so horrified that a British Colonel could be regarded in such a manner, that they brought pressure to bear on Laurence Olivier, who was then serving in the Fleet Air Arm, and had been offered the role. They advised him that it would do neither the national cause, nor his career, much good if he accepted. So the script was re-written and toned down to a great extent, and Roger Livesey donned Olivier's 'Sam Browne'. Livesey gave an entirely new and individualistic interpretation of the character, turning him into a bumbling, sentimental old buffoon. The public loved him, the Low fans didn't recognize him, and Winston Churchill, who went to the

99

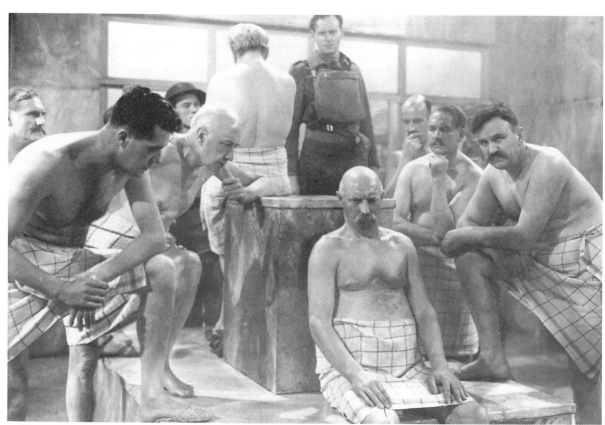

film's première, thought it 'disgraceful'. Powell claimed that, although on the whole the film was a public success, he would still have preferred Olivier in the role. His partner, Pressburger, who did much of the redrafting of the screenplay, however, was delighted with the result, and especially with Livesey's fine performance.

The story concerns Clive Wynn Candy (Roger Livesey), a young Boer War VC who goes to Berlin to trap a German spy. He becomes friends with the German officer, Theo (Anton Walbrook), after they fight a duel, which is brought about by German accusations of British atrocities committed against the Boers. This was probably the part that Churchill detested the most, as he had been a young officer serving in that war himself. Candy and Theo become such good friends, in fact, that Theo steals the girl to whom Candy was about to propose. But in the 1914 War, Candy meets another girl who reminds him of his first lost love, and this time he slaps the ring on her finger pretty damned quick, or at least fast by his standards. At the outset of the Second World War, Candy is now a widower, and his old duelling chum Theo has come to live at his house, as an anti-Hitler refugee vouched for by Candy. Having been axed from the Army, Brigadier-General Wynn Candy becomes a leader of the Home Guard. Before a planned exercise begins, Candy is captured in the Turkish bath of his club by a young officer, who on his own initiative has decided to start his 'war' before midnight and not at midnight, as laid down by Candy. Furious at this young officer's impertinence, Candy threatens to break him, but is dissuaded from doing so by Theo, and Candy realizes that 'total war' needs totally modern ideas. A young Deborah Kerr became a star, playing all the loves of Candy's life – his lost first love, his wife, and later as his driver in the ATS.

The Life and Death of Colonel Blimp was an expensive and ambitious film. Shot in Technicolor, a rarity for wartime productions, it also ran for 163 minutes, well over an hour longer than the average feature-film length. Despite mixed reactions at the time, the film has now taken on a sort of cult status. Martin Scorsese, the noted American film director, says that when he saw the film as a young man it had a profound effect on him, and admits that the build-up to the duel sequence in the gymnasium, with its almost ritualistic and religious quality, influenced the way he directed the much-acclaimed *Raging Bull*, and as a result he decided to show very little of the actual fight scenes.

The importance being given by the MoI to the role played by women in the War – both as members of the forces and in industry, resulted in a whole spate of British films charting their new and vital contribution to the struggle, and injecting into the storylines the idea that working in factories and other essential services also had an element of glamour attached to it. *Millions Like Us* (1943) was typical of this type of propaganda, making the showbiz personnel at the MoI beam from ear to ear, and shout 'encore' to our busy studios. 'This is the sort of stuff that helps to win wars,' they seemed to say, 'not all that Blimp poppycock.'

Phyllis Calvert, Renee Houston, Patricia Roc and Flora Robson in *2000 Women*, 1944

Millions Like Us was written and directed by Frank Launder and Sidney Gilliat, and was the only film the famous twosome ever directed side by side on the floor. It was an account of two girls working in an aircraft factory, shot in documentary style, with the emphasis on the message of the moment. It focused firmly on their love relationships, but thrown in for good measure was a cross-fertilization of class, as an 'upper-class' young lady (Ann Crawford) is drafted into the factory on essential war work, and in spite of her snobbish upbringing falls head over spanner in love with the foreman (Eric Portman), whilst a down-to-earth working-class lass (Patricia Roc) meets and marries a boy in the Air Force (Gordon Jackson) representing the middle class. Basil Radford and Naunton Wayne as Army officers, performing with their usual upper-class eccentricity, give the film some lighter moments.

Just before his death on a flight from Lisbon in 1943, Leslie Howard made his own personal statement on women at war by directing *The Gentle Sex*. This time the women were members of the Auxiliary Territorial Service. The story covers the lives of seven girls who are all from different backgrounds, and who meet for the first time on a train. The introduction to the film is by Leslie Howard himself, picking out the principal players amongst crowds of real servicemen and women on Victoria Station. After that we follow their activities as they are processed through actual ATS training centres. Of the seven young girls featured in the film, Rosamund John, Joan Greenwood and Lili Palmer (playing a Czech refugee) went on to distinguish themselves as fine film actresses.

It needs to be recorded that the film-makers of the time also produced some spectacularly silly epics – films such as the totally implausible 2,000 Women (1944), which stars Patricia Roc, Phyllis Calvert, Flora Robson and Renée Houston. It is set in a women's internment camp in Paris, formerly a top-class hotel. They organize themselves into tight little groups of campaigning ladies whose aim, apparently, is to do their utmost to upset the 'Jerry' guards, help two RAF airmen who have baled out near the camp to escape (shades of Allo, Allo – the BBC situation comedy series of some forty years later), and generally parade around in French underwear. The glamorous Jean Kent, in silk stockings and camiknickers, plays the sexiest parader of them all. With Patricia Roc cast as a nun on the run, it was, to put it mildly, a little hard to swallow. But if it was intended to please servicemen on leave, especially the scene where Phyllis Calvert practically bares her all, then it was presumably a resounding success.

Lili Palmer in _The Gentle Sex_, 1943

Henry V, 1944

Laurence Olivier in *Henry V*, 1944

Other war films aimed straight for the funnybone, and were produced purely as vehicles for music-hall comedians, like the Crazy Gang in *Gas Bags* (1940), all intended to ridicule the nasty Nazis (see chapter 4). But every aspect of music and drama was explored and exploited by the film-makers in an effort to boost our morale without boring us to distraction – because towards the end of the War, the British cinema public was beginning to tire of films that dealt solely with the chaps at sea, above and below the waves, the boys in light blue buzzing around in the sky, and the lads in khaki being square-bashed by the barking sergeant major with the heart of gold. In our darkest hour we wanted, more than anything, to be entertained; to be removed, however briefly, from the grim situation we were in, not constantly reminded of it.

The producers now had to strike a balance: propaganda as decreed by the MoI still had to be very much in evidence, of course, but now the medicine was to be sweetened with nice sugary love, music, comedy and even culture. When Laurence Olivier went into production in 1944 with William Shakespeare's *Henry V*, it was, as far as the MoI was concerned, more than a cultural exercise; for parallels could be drawn very vividly with the Allied Forces' invasion of Normandy, on what was known to the British public as the 'Second Front', and to the Allied Chiefs of Staff under the code name of 'Overlord'. In *Henry V* the King is seen setting forth for his invasion of Normandy some 500 years before the Allied attack. With his army of 30,000 men, which includes 2,500 men at arms, 8,000 archers and a fleet of 1,500 ships, he sets off from Southampton. The medieval warriors encounter much the same difficulties as their descendants experienced hundreds of years later – sea-sickness on the English Channel, being crammed like sardines in tins in their armada of vessels, and the problems of getting weapons ashore when they are landing. In Henry V's time, it was horses, carts, armour and food supplies. During the Allied invasion, it was heavy artillery, vehicles and goods supplies.

Most of the exterior scenes for *Henry V* were shot in Eire, because the landscape was uncluttered with telegraph poles and other twentieth-century devices; also because the extras in Eire would work for £3.10s.0d a week, and a quid more if they rode and brought their own horse. Olivier, although an officer in the Fleet Air Arm at the time, was not used to commanding such numbers of men, and here he was having to marshal and direct more than 700 tough Irishmen. He decided that he would show them who was boss from the outset and, addressing them from the top of a beer crate, told them that he was going to ask them to perform some tricky stuff, especially during the battle scenes, but nothing that he would not, or could not, do himself. He got a mighty round of applause for this piece of bravado.

Later on the same day, he required about two dozen extras to climb up into the trees and, on the word 'action' leap down on to the knights as they rode beneath them, and drag them from their horses. As he was relaying his request, and reassuring the extras that this was just a simple stunt, he observed a few nods and knowing winks pass between them. He was slightly taken aback

106

when one of the extras piped up, 'That sounds just fine, Mr Olivier – but we would like to see you do it first.' Not wishing to lose credibility, Olivier had no choice but to attempt it. Shinning up a tree, he waited for the stunt rider to pass beneath him. All was going well until the final fall, when he felt a stabbing pain in his foot. He was in agaony but, putting on a brave face, he turned to the men and said through gritted teeth, 'See, it's easy really.'

The men seemed satisfied, and started to make preparations, while Olivier limped out of sight behind a big tree and cried in pain like a baby. The film was dedicated 'to all those serving in the Second World War,' and if ever a demonstration of fighting spirit against enormous odds were needed, surely there was no better example that that given by Olivier himself.

Each of the Armed Services had at least one memorable feature film to represent it in all its glory. In the case of the Air Force it was *The Way to the Stars* (1945), the Army had *The Way Ahead* (1944), whilst the Navy had *We Dive at Dawn* (1943), and the Senior Service landmark film, *In Which We Serve*.

John Mills in *We Dive at Dawn*, 1943

The Way to the Stars, written by Terrence Rattigan, directed by Anthony Asquith and starring Michael Redgrave, John Mills, Rosamond John, Douglass Montgomery and Renée Asherson, was a sensitive treatment of the delicate relationship between the RAF and the USAF. It went beyond the blood and guts and nerves-of-steel dogfight scenes, to examine the far deeper emotional aspects of the lives of these airmen from both sides of the Atlantic: their loves, hopes and dreams at the concluding stages of the War. The script, as one would expect from Rattigan, made profound statements with which cinema audiences of the period could identify very closely. Making their film débuts were Jean Simmons, as a rather precocious singer, Bonar Colleano, and another young actor, with whom John Mills had been so thrilled at playing a scene that he rushed home to his wife (the playwright Mary Hayley Bell), and told her he was convinced 'that chap' would become a big star. 'That chap' did not let him down; he went on to become a star of international reputation – his name, Trevor Howard. *The Way to the Stars* also contained two poems specially written for it by John Pudney, which gave the story an additional lyrical quality. One was called 'Missing', and the other 'Johnny in the Sky', the last poignant verse of which read:

> Better by far,
> For Johnny – the bright star,
> To keep your head
> And see his children fed.

Anthony Asquith, who liked to 'tipple' sometimes more than was wise, walked alongside the camera as it tracked John Mills, who himself was walking and reciting the verse. While he was keeping his eyes on Mills's performance all through the shot, Asquith walked straight into a brick wall. He apologised at once to the wall – his manners were always impeccable.

The Way Ahead was directed by one of Britain's all-time greats – Carol Reed. It starred David Niven, William Hartnell, Stanley Holloway and Raymond Huntley – and all of them gave splendid performances. There were certain similarities in the opening storyline to that of *The Gentle Sex*. We encounter a group of civilians who have been called up as they converge on a railway station, and on the train journey to their destination we observe the widely divergent backgrounds from which the recruits are drawn. We listen to their very firm views on life and the situation they find themselves in – all are late and unwilling conscripts.

They are put through rigorous training over a period of several weeks by their drill sergeant (William Hartnell), and eventually, after a lot of sweat, tears and heartache, they become a tight, efficient fighting body of men, ready to do battle in North Africa, and the pride and joy of their CO played by David Niven. The script was by a writer who went on to distinguish himself as a master of spy fiction – Eric Ambler. His co-writer was a very young Peter Ustinov, who also played a scene in the film as the French speaking proprietor of a North African bar. (In reality he was, at the time of making the film, Private Ustinov, batman to the star, David Niven.)

Kenneth More in *Reach for the Sky*, 1956

John Mills in *We Dive at Dawn*, 1943

Some two years before directing *The Way to the Stars*, Anthony Asquith had made another contribution to wartime feature films by plunging to the depths of the sea with *We Dive at Dawn* (1943), in tribute to the submarine service. Asquith would have seemed a most unlikely candidate for a major film director, having been brought up at No. 10 Downing Street, the son of the Liberal Prime Minister. But he had rejected a political career at a very early age, opting instead to become a composer. In the event, he was an extremely unsuccessful composer, and changed his affections from music to the cinema. In this field he found his feet. Anthony 'Puffin' (the nick-name his mother gave him because of his flattish nose) Asquith's name will always be synonymous in the film industry with 'style' – not surprising, really, for he had this in his private and working life in abundance.

In the documentary vein so approved of by the MoI, *We Dive at Dawn* charts the story of a submarine crew on the trail of, and finally hunting down and attacking a new Nazi battleship. Then – and this is the main thrust of the film – the submarine tries to return through hostile waters, to a safe port. The film stars John Mills as the submarine commander, and he did his homework for the part by going out with a submarine crew and learning how to crash-dive, and to use the periscope. All crews in the submarine service were volunteers during the War, and they were, Mills reflects, the finest and friendliest body of men he had ever encountered. He later went on to prove his admiration for them by making two further films about the submarine service.

During the Second World War, the British film industry justified all the faith and confidence that the MoI had in it. In terms of raising our morale, they were second to none, for they spoke to us in a way that we all understood. They rarely preached. If this meant that at times they did glorify war, it was to demonstrate that to lay down one's life for a cause that one truly believed in – in this case freedom and democracy – could be, and was, ultimately justified.

8

Power and Prejudice

As the British people picked up the pieces of their lives in the difficult years immediately following the War, so the movies they went to see began to reflect the social attitudes, struggles and problems that ordinary people had to deal with in their austere ration-book existence.

A new Labour government was in power, and the country's population looked to it for signs of dramatic improvement. Two World Wars, a General Strike, low wages, unemployment, inadequate housing and food shortages had left the people reeling. Coupled with the newly acquired knowledge that in America, our 'cousins' seemed to live a life of endless money and opportunity.

So, in an atmosphere of uneasy expectancy, Britain sought to rebuild itself. *This Happy Breed* was one of the first British films to be 'epic' in feel. Although essentially a small saga of one family, it spans twenty years and three generations, and is representative of the turmoil of the nation. From the viewpoint of the Gibbons household, we see the upheavals of the 1920s and 1930s. The General Strike, the Depression, the death of George V, plus the growing dissatisfaction of youth and the craving for something more. The film is based on Noel Coward's play and is remarkably faithful to it, preferring to stay inside the Gibbons house and tell the story through the emotional responses of the characters as each event occurs, and as it affects their daily routine.

Frank Gibbons (Robert Newton) returns home after the amnesty of 1918 and settles with his wife and children in Clapham, a suburb of London. As their daughters reach womanhood, one of them, Queenie (Kay Walsh) runs away from home with a married man. In 1944 the idea, never mind the reality, of a young daughter having an affair with a married man was deeply shocking. To see the effect this incident has on the Gibbons household is both a surprise for the modern viewer and enormously moving. Ethel, her mother, literally disowns her, and Frank is left in despair at losing his daughter and the realization that his wife has rejected Queenie for her unforgivable sins.

C.A. Lejeune, the respected film critic, at the time writing for the *Observer*, noted that Noel Coward, who cared more about the Navy's opinion of *In Which We Serve* (see chapter 7) than the critics' approval, must have felt a glow of satisfaction over the release of *This Happy Breed*, for this film about the suburbs had gone out into the suburbs, and they had taken it to their hearts. All the Gibbonses of Greater London flocked to see themselves on the screen. People in fish queues, fruit queues, bus queues, and queues for queues, passed the word to each other over their baskets. They were amused, touched, entertained and edified all at once. It went

This Happy Breed, 1944

straight to their address – or, as they say sometimes, genteelly in their suburbs, *Chez Nous*. The whole is an essential 'photo' for John Bull's family album.

In the story, Queenie's attempt to find romance and prosperity is brought to an end in Marseilles, when the young sailor who lives next door, and who loves her, finds her and brings her home. Although she isn't grateful, it may be that she loves the young sailor (John Mills), but he is still poor, working-class and ordinary. Queenie's mother Ethel (Celia Johnson) still disowns her, and a family rift is spawned. Frank and Ethel's other children, Vi and Reg, become entangled with a young socialist and the family is further fractured. Soon there are grandchildren, born as the shadow of the second Great War looms overhead.

This Happy Breed was the first solo directorial effort of David Lean, who went on to become one of Britian's most influential and internationally appreciated directors. More than forty years on, he is still active. His recent film *A Passage to India* (1984) is the latest in a series of epics that tell stories on a huge visual scale. *Bridge on the River Kwai* (1957), *Lawrence of Arabia* (1962) and *Dr Zhivago* (1965) are three classic examples of Lean's cinema – and their impact on a younger generation of film-makers is very keenly felt. American whizz-kid Steven Spielberg (*Jaws*, *Raiders of the Lost Ark*, *ET* and so on) claims that Lean's films so excited him as a teenager that he spent hours in his bedroom trying to re-create them with his 8mm home-movie camera! In fact, *The Colour Purple* (1985) clearly demonstrates Spielberg's love for Lean's work, paying direct homage to *Dr Zhivago*, a movie where the central characters often viewed their world through frosted, iced or rain-splattered windows. This is a recurring image in Lean's art, and early in *This Happy Breed* there is a stunning shot, as the camera pans across the rooftops of rows and rows of terraced houses – and finally enters the Gibbons house through a rear window. Continuing to move, the camera tracks across the landing and all the way down the stairs. It reaches the front door, which opens, admitting the Gibbons family.

Although *This Happy Breed* is historically superficial, and somewhat trivializes important issues of the day, it handles sentiment well, which was Noel Coward's trademark. And the performances are particularly convincing, especially those of Robert Newton and Celia Johnson, who make you feel their anguish as parents trying to protect their children from destructive elements. And above all there is David Lean, whose fusing of emotion and technique works superbly in the scene where Vi (the eldest daughter) has to tell her mum and dad that Reg has just been killed in a car crash. They are in the garden and Vi hesitates in the dining room. She plucks up the nerve and moves outside. On the screen is an empty room and we wait, curious but afraid. After a long pause, Ethel enters, followed by Frank. They sit, and only then does Lean cut to Frank, gently placing his hand on his wife's hand. Then we back away – and the screen fades to black. Lean was much helped by the lush colour photography of cameraman Ronald Neame, and together they created in *This Happy Breed* a visual hymn to the working-class ethos which contributed to Rank's, and the film industry's, advance to a new social realism.

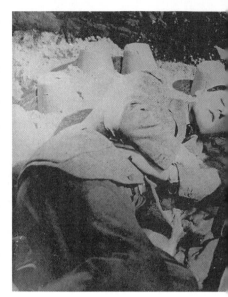

above, Margaret Lockwood in *Bank Holiday*, 1938

Another British director of enormous talent and influence, with a penchant for socially disturbing films, was at this time honing his skills and preparing to deliver three of the greatest films ever made. Carol Reed (who was knighted in 1952) had been directing since the early 1930s, and had come to the attention of the filmgoers in 1938 with the release of his quite controversial *Bank Holiday*. This film was constructed on the *Grand Hotel* principle, whereby a number of characters with different stories are woven in and out of an episodic plot. It really centres on a young nurse, Catherine (Margaret Lockwood), who has a boyfriend, Geoffrey (Hugh Williams), with whom she is intending to spend an illicit weekend in a plush seaside hotel. However, this is made trickier by her becoming emotionally involved with a young man at the hospital, whose wife has just died in childbirth.

David Lean directing *This Happy Breed*, 1944

Of course, in 1938, the idea of an unmarried couple spending time in a hotel double bedroom was pretty hair-raising. But the puritans needn't have worried, because the issue is fudged in a particularly innocuous fashion, as the boyfriend, overcome by nerves, botches the booking horribly. His enquiries – such as 'Does the 18/6d price include breakfast?' – are smoothly glossed over by an overpolite clerk, who kindly diffuses embarrassment by informing the nervous couple that as far as doubles are concerned, there's no room at the inn.

Bank Holiday begins with masses of people knocking off work and joining long queues at Victoria Station. Regardless of occupation, it appears that everyone is going to get away from it all. The attitude is carefree. But the man who waits alone at the hospital, Stephen Howard (John Lodge), is suffering anguish that no holiday could cure. His emotional, and subsequently physical, isolation dominates the film. It is his character that interests Reed most, and it is the forerunner of the obsessive loners who will figure in his later films. However, the doom-laden aspects of *Bank Holiday* are lightened by

above right, Kathleen Harrison in *Bank Holiday*, 1938

right, Patricia Roc and Torin Thatcher in *When the Bough Breaks*, 1947

some comic moments, featuring Wally Patch and Kathleen Harrison as a typical pair of cockney oiks with a barrel-load of kids causing mayhem and getting lost.

The film really comes to life in crowd scenes. Reed shows a real genius at integrating with, or isolating against, the hurly-burly those characters who are most relevant to his plot. It is, as C.A. Lejeune wrote at the time, an improbable story which has been given, through the truth of its detail, an air of almost indisputable authenticity. The film had its share of controversy, too, over a scene where Margaret Lockwood tries to commit suicide by putting her head in a gas oven. Frank Launder, the producer, remembers that the censor said that he could not pass this, and showed him a letter he had received years earlier from the Gas, Light & Coke Company, as it was then, protesting about an incident in an Alfred Hitchcock film where the heroine had attempted suicide by a similar means.

The Gas Company complained that, when the film went on release in Britain, numbers of love-lorn maidens had started putting their heads in gas ovens. This was a very worrying problem, because it meant that people were changing to electricity...

In its way, *Bank Holiday* is an important British film, and it has been compared to early Hitchcock. It is not afraid to be experimental in its use of flashbacks (uncommon at the time), and in mixing locations with studio material.

A quotation at the end of *Bank Holiday* reads: 'No more let death dwell where two are joined together'. This is from Shelley's 'Adonais', and could equally be applied to the film that opened Carol Reed's golden period. *Odd Man Out* (1947) was the first of three consecutive Carol Reed films to garner British Academy Awards for Best Picture. The others were *The Fallen Idol* (1948) and *The Third Man* (1949). *Odd Man Out* is the ultimate 'escape' movie. In the ever-increasing desire to change the face of the social landscape, the hero, or anti-hero, of the film, Johnny McQueen (James Mason), dreams of the 'cause' and raising funds for the 'organization'. In the shady back streets of an Irish town, Johnny is a leader. Only there's a problem: his insistence on leading his men on a raid to acquire more money for the cause is ill judged, and the consequences affect the lives of many of those around him. At the beginning of the film, Johnny's men are expressing doubts about his ability to carry out the heist. Recently, he has spent time in prison, and has been hiding away in rooms with the blinds drawn, avoiding neighbours and the police. He is unfit suddenly to rush into the crowded streets masterminding a robbery. But, eager to prove he is still the best man for the job, Johnny ignores their warnings, and disaster waits round the corner. At a crucial moment during the robbery, Johnny is beset by a dizzy spell and holds up the escape. As he struggles, gunfire erupts, he unintentionally murders his assailant, and he is also wounded. Left alone, he wanders through the alleys seriously hurt, while his girlfriend Kathleen (Kathleen Ryan) strives to find him before the police.

What marks *Odd Man Out* as an astounding achievement is the extraordinary atmosphere generated by Robert Krasker's black-and-white photography. The haunting imagery becomes almost surreal as the life literally drains out of Johnny. The mood is chilling. Johnny's last hours are full of pain, both mental and physical. He reflects on the nature of violence, and in one hallucinatory scene, quotes from the Book of Corinthians –, 'When I was a child, I spake as a child ... ', concluding: 'And now abideth faith, hope, charity, these three, and the greatest of these is charity ... ' Johnny understands the urges that have brought him to this point, and the implications of the quotation, but the self-knowledge has come too late to save him.

Reed's direction is masterly, and the actors playing characters who have fleeting contact with Johnny on his way to oblivion give unbeatable performances, many of them coming from the famous Abbey Theatre in Dublin. It is a brave film, which opens with a caption. It reads: 'This story is told against a background of political unrest in a city of Northern Ireland. It is not concerned with the

James Mason and Kathleen Ryan in *Odd Man Out*, 1946

inset, James Mason in *Odd Man Out*, 1946

114

struggle between the law and an illegal organisation, but only with the conflict in the hearts of the people when they become unexpectedly involved.'

For Carol Reed, it has always been the human element that fascinates, coupled with constant spontaneity. The first shot of James Mason, wounded and running across deserted ground to hide in a shelter, included a dog following the man. Reed did not hesitate to use the take, and from that day and for the entire shoot the owner, a ten-year-old girl, turned up every morning in case her little dog was needed again.

Kathleen Ryan's 'heroic' sacrifice at the climax of the film has been shrouded in controversy. Reed wanted her to shoot Mason, but friends advised that this action would create a censorship dilemma in th US, because it would be a murder in order to allow her lover to escape justice. The answer was surely to let the police shoot him while he was trying to escape. Reed was not happy, but eventually found the answer. Kathy seems to fire at the police, who in reply shoot both Mason and herself. However, it is made quite clear that she has actually shot at the ground.

Odd Man Out remains an unforgettable experience for anyone who sees it – and it is deservedly thought of as one of Britain's finest films. Indeed, in a recent conversation the Hollywood director Fred Zinneman (*High Noon*, *From Here to Eternity*) stated that in his opinion *Odd Man Out* was very possibly the best so far, the most outstanding that the British industry has yet produced. There is a deep sadness about the ending, even though we presumably believe that Kathleen's love for Johnny transcends life itself and can continue in a future existence. It was a rarity in the 1940s for women on film to be able to precipitate a change in a man's destiny in this fashion. It was more usual to see women as stoically suffering victims, cruelly treated by their men, and having to hold heart and home together on a shoestring budget. Any attempt at independent thinking was forcefully quashed by male authoritarian figures and the women would be 'corrected' in an institution, or remain 'fallen' for ever.

Patricia Roc suffers gamely as a young mum, in *When the Bough Breaks* (1947), who, whilst nursing her newborn baby in hospital, is informed by the police that her husband is a bigamist. This film, directed by Lawrence Huntington, and with a screenplay by Peter Rogers (later to find fame, as the producer of the 'Carry On' series – see chapter 4) manages to combine a helpless woman with the working-class aspirations of 'betterment', significant in the climate of the time. Lily (Patricia Roc) continues to work by placing her growing son Jimmy in a day nursery. There, he is coveted by a wealthy voluntary worker, Mrs Norman (Rosamund John), who finally persuades Lily to allow her to adopt Jimmy. Lily agrees, but doesn't sign any legal papers. Several years later, after Lily has married a plain, dull, but honourable shopkeeper (Bill Owen) they recover Jimmy through the courts. However, Jimmy finds problems in readjusting to his working-class status, and is eventually returned to Mrs Norman and the affluent society.

above and below, Jean Kent in *Good Time Girl*, 1948

In 1947 critics were divided over *When the Bough Breaks*. ' ... A woman producer (Betty Box) is responsible for the British film surprise packet of the year ... ' wrote the *Daily Worker* in November of that year, concluding that ' ... (It's) a fine piece of filmcraft that should reap dividends at the box office.' The *Observer* took a different view; C.A. Lejeune, an acidic person at the best of times, decided the film was worth an award: 'I intend to revive the Lejeune lemon ...' he wrote magnanimously. 'It's a long time since I have been able to award this ripe, luscious, full-flavoured fruit to a British picture, but never did a piece of nonsense merit it more radiantly ... A supreme example of imbecility.' Still, undeterred by Lejeune's impromptu 'Oscar', the Box team, Betty and husband Sydney, ploughed straight into another production – and into more controversy. *Good Time Girl* (1948) jumped right into the seedy side of life. Petty larceny, reform schools, low-life nightclubs; and all involving a young woman!

Here was the story of the girl of the title, Jean Kent, struggling to escape, but not legitimately. First she is beaten by her father because she has been sacked supposedly for stealing. Forced to leave home, she settles in a run-down boarding house. A fellow lodger (Jimmy), a waiter, gets her a job in a slummy nightclub. But Gwen (Jean Kent) is of course attractive, and comes under the amorous scrutiny of Max (Herbert Lom), the night-club boss. Inevitably Max and Jimmy argue over Gwen, and Jimmy is fired. He swears he'll get even. He persuades Gwen to pawn stolen jewellery; she is then arrested in the flat of a 'fence', Red Farrell (Dennis Price), and she is tried, found guilty and sent to an approved school for three years. Inside she fights the other girls – and authority! Gwen, despite her spirit and strength of character, is on the slippery slope – and her decline will be total.

Sydney and Betty Box were determined to make a realistic film that would tackle the question of problem girls in British cities, and the present state of 'approved schools'. Betty Box was convinced that the system of correction and punishment for youngsters was not working. For her troubles, the film's release was held up for over a year. The Home Office studied the film and its ramifications and demanded that their officials and psychiatrists should have private showings. A mountain of paperwork resulted, and eventually specific censorship demands were made. The Boxes had to make cuts, but none the less a worthwhile drama was released.

Good Time Girl was a realistic and shocking film for its day. Once more, a 'family' film divided the critics, and once again C.A. Lejeune stuck the knife in:

'It's a squalid film about a young woman from a bad home who gets into the company of thieves, seducers, drunkards, black marketeers, army deserters, razor slashers and vitriol throwers, and ends up with 15 years for murder. It is not the sort of film I like and I like it none the better because it is presented with a smug complacency that seems to be the last resort of hypocritical cant, as a cautionary tale within a tale.'

But the *Monthly Film Bulletin* defended it: 'Tensely gripping in its seamiest situations, it holds the interest to the end and makes the heart beat faster ... It is not for the squeamish or for those who prefer seeing the world through rose coloured spectacles.' *Good Time Girl* was a bold enterprise, aiming to show people how easy it was (or is) to degrade oneself in the struggle to escape the poverty trap.

Turn the Key Softly (1953) attempted to take things further. Again dealing with convicted women, it centres on the story of three female prisoners, all released on the same day. They are three very distinct types. First, there is Monica (Yvonne Mitchell), whose lover had made her assist him in a housebreaking, then absconded when the police arrived, leaving her to face the music. Next is Stella (a youthful Joan Collins), a high-class prostitute, now reformed, who intends to marry a bus conductor, and Mrs Quilliam (Kathleen Harrison), who steals small items from shops, and cares only for her dog, Johnny. Rather improbably, the three meet twenty-four hours later for a reunion in a restaurant, and discuss their hopes and fears.

As it turns out, despite her efforts to go straight, Monica's husband deceives her again. Stella flirts with her old career, before finally settling for the conductor. Mrs Quilliam sadly loses her dog, and is run over looking for him. Eventually a lonely Monica retrieves the dog and takes him home. Although a valiant idea, this film never takes off, because of a very ponderous script. Its contrivances and implausibilities defeat the direction.

What *When the Bough Breaks, Good Time Girl* and *Turn the Key Softly* deomonstrate is the unwillingness of realistic ideas of society to come together filmically whilst conforming to the narrow censorship of the 1940s and 1950s. It would be another decade or so before realism really began to materialize.

And its shape was the curved ball of the rugby prop forward. Literally kicked across the screen with all the hate, fury and pent-up frustration that Frank Machin could muster. Machin, as portrayed by the exciting newcomer Richard Harris, could express all the discontent of the trapped working classes with one lunge of his powerful frame. Leaving a ruck of scrambling players behind, Frank accelerates clear – all the way to the goal line.

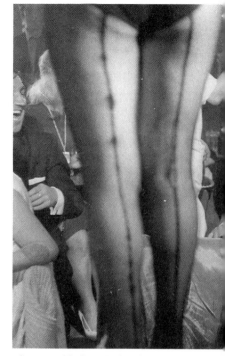

above and below, Richard Harris in *This Sporting Life*, 1963

Yvonne Mitchell, Kathleen Harrison, Joan Collins in *Turn the Key Softly*, 1953

Stanley Baker in *Violent Playground*, 1958

This Sporting Life (1963) was a real breakthrough. Here was the way to 'escape' all right. From lowly miner to top-paid rugby footballer, Frank crunches his way out. And all you can hear are the screams, and the sound of values being broken underfoot. Frank is a young miner, who rooms with Mrs Hammond (Rachel Roberts), a widow with two young children. But Frank has ambition. He can play the great game and he intends to be the best. An old scout for the club, Johnson (William Hartnell), has faith in Frank, and persuades the City Club to give him a trial. Frank's skill and evident love of brutality impress Weaver, the club's owner. Frank is signed, and he receives a cheque for £1,000. Unbelievable money. Frank hopes that Mrs Hammond will warm to him. She doesn't. In fact she seems more aggressive, more antagonistic; she belittles Frank's money by saying it's more that her husband's life was worth. When he died in a pit accident, there was hardly any compensation. Frank's failure to win her over only results in his becoming cruder and rougher, but eventually she softens. Frank resists the advances of an industrialist's wife, and with it the 'good life'. But his relationship with the intransigent Mrs Hammond only worsens, culminating in her death from a brain haemorrhage. Frank is shattered, and torn by remorse, but he recovers to find even more brutal strength on the rugby pitch.

This Sporting Life was the highly acclaimed feature début of the director Lindsay Anderson, whose early documentaries – *Idlers That Work* (1949), *Wakefield Express* (1952), *Green and Pleasant Land* (1955) – were poignant commentaries on English working-class existence. It seemed natural then, that he would turn to features, and perhaps no one was surprised at the ferocity that the film conveyed. The performances are uniformly good. Richard Harris especially as bull-headed Frank, and the latent sadness that underpins Rachel Roberts's steely, resolute, 'in-control' Mrs Hammond. Also William Hartnell and Colin Blakely, who support Frank through his darkest hours, and Alan Badel, as the slippery-smooth Weaver, the epitome of middle-class aspiration.

Lindsay Anderson has never really found his niche in contemporary British cinema. Maybe he is too uncomfortable for the Establishment. But after *This Sporting Life* he delivered a trilogy that would be deservedly sought after by any nation's film industry,

Stanley Baker in *Violent Playground*, 1958

If (1968), *O Lucky Man* (1973) and *Britannia Hospital* (1982) – three films that charted a country's disillusionment, finally breaking down completely in a welter of strikes and unemployment. These austere pictures of Britain in decay aren't the most pleasant viewing, but their essential truth, presented by a film-maker who cares, cannot be ignored.

As the increasingly socially aware 1950s had progressed, other themes had come sharply into focus: the law, juvenile delinquency and racialism. Two films from the prolific producing/directing team of Michael Relph and Basil Dearden, tentatively studied these issues. The first, *Violent Playground* (1958), is set in Liverpool. A city beginning to find its feel after the War, but containing many Irish and black immigrants and the bombed-out slums that still pitted the city's vistas like open sores, and conspired to create tensions that would one day (in the 1980s) explode. The reluctant hero of *Violent Playground* is a policeman, Det.-Sgt Truman, played by Stanley Baker. He is taken off a series of arson cases and transferred to the new junior liaison division.

The subject at the crux of the film is 'The Great Experiment' introduced by the Chief Constable of Liverpool in 1949, and since copied throughout the world – the Juvenile Liaison Officers'

Scheme – which, in simple terms, meant that at the discretion of a police officer, a boy or girl under seventeen who admits a first minor offence need not appear before a magistrate, but is consequently put in the officer's charge. In 1958 it had been 98 per cent successful, although policemen like Det.-Sgt Truman had their patience tried by children who soon began to understand it was quite simple to get away with a first offence – as a really young child says to him, 'You can't frame me, I'm not eight yet!'

Although dealing with kids doesn't seem to be his forte, Truman battles on gamely. One of his duties is keeping a watchful eye on the young Murphy twins. In doing so, he gets to know their older brother, Johnny, who is a gang leader. Furthermore, he suspects Johnny of being an arsonist. Spending more and more time in the Murphy home, because he has fallen in love with Cathy Murphy (Anne Heywood), Truman becomes convinced, in his suspicions. Johnny, cornered and dangerous, believes he has been betrayed by his sister; he takes a class of children hostage in a classroom. Eventually he gives himself up – persuaded by the quiet tones of Cathy.

Violent Playground is, generally speaking, an honourable attempt at portraying the problems which were rapidly arising in Britain's inner cities. Stanley Baker is always watchable, and he brings to Truman a humanity (almost a naivety) that makes him very sympathetic. And if today's entrenched audiences would not accept its simplistic statements of life, love and the law, this is not to say that those people who witnessed *Violent Playground* on first release should be denigrated for an acceptance of a world that was not quite the 'Violent Playground' then that it is now.

Michael Craig and Nigel Patrick in
Sapphire, 1959

Dearden and Relph had more success (both critical and commercial) with the second effort, *Sapphire* (1959). This was a full-blooded examination of racial unease, and it was rewarded with a British Academy Award for Best Film.

A music student, Sapphire Robbins, is murdered. Although she was thought to be white, she was in fact half black. Now the investigation, led by Det.-Supt Hazzard (Nigel Patrick) and his sidekick, Sgt Learoyd (Michael Craig), homes in on London's West Indian population. The film characterizes very well the twilight world that exists for the half-caste, and the difficulties of being accepted by black or white. *Sapphire* is photographed, in colour, by the much under-rated British cameraman, Harry Waxman, and he achieves some remarkable contrasts of light and shade. Each environment seems atmospherically different, from eerie alleyways at night to the harsh, flat interiors of seedy boarding houses in the cold light of day. Basil Dearden's direction has an energy in *Sapphire* not matched in his other work. Although condemned by several critics for being unconvincing and unnecessarily melodramatic, *Sapphire* is a thriller with a sharp bite. And as the jaws close around the film's killer (a white woman superbly played by Yvonne Mitchell), there is a concern for the issues at stake and a compassion that still touches the viewer.

John Mills, Sylvia Sims and Earl Cameron in *Flame in the Streets*, 1961

Sapphire's success paved the way for other forays into racial unrest at the beginning of the 1960s. The sensitivity of the subject led perhaps inevitably to tentative handling, usually culminating in melodrama. *Flame in the Street* (1961) is typical of this approach, despite its good intentions. As Britain was struggling to come to terms with the growing cosmopolitanism of the major cities, the knock-on effect for the younger generation was the most profound. Mixing with the other races was unavoidable anyway, either in the schools or on the streets, so some of the kids found it wasn't all antagonism. But, when love came, so did a whole set of different problems. *Flame in the Street* was adapted from his own stage play, *Hot Summer Night*, by Ted Willis.

The story's main protagonist is Jacko Palmer (John Mills), a craftsman in a furniture factory who is well known for his union work and liberal attitudes. He always supports the appointment of 'coloured' employees, and he persuades the union to give Gomez (Earl Cameron), a West Indian, a job as a chargehand. But later Jacko is badly shocked when his wife Nell (Brenda de Banzie) informs him that their daughter Kathie has fallen for a Jamaican called Peter Lincoln (Johnny Sekka), and wants to marry him. Faced with the probable consequences of such a disastrous 'union', Nell borders on breakdown – and, turning on Jacko, she bitterly berates him for putting his outside activities before the family. Shaken by his wife's outburst, he tries to talk Peter out of marrying Kathie, but this only confirms their resolve to go ahead. It is only when Gomez is beaten up by Teddy boys that Jacko relents and accepts the inevitable.

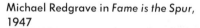

Michael Redgrave in *Fame is the Spur*, 1947

Sapphire and *Flame in the Streets* opened up endless arguments on the subject of immigrant communities in England. They came about as the result of the fast-emerging 'immigrant question' and

above right, Michael Craig in
Sapphire, 1959

right, Earl Cameron in *Flame in the
Streets*, 1961

below right, Michael Redgrave and
Rosamund John in *Fame is the Spur*,
1947

one could see, through reaction to both the films, British society's firm resistance to any change in terms of black cultural realities. *Flame in the Streets* literally called a spade a spade, and *Sapphire* demanded whether London could really be like this – do landladies who find a coloured man on the doorstep react as if stricken by the plague and say: 'I'm sorry, I keep a white house. I have my living to think of?' Do policeman say: 'These spades are all the same, a load of trouble. They should all be sent back where they belong.?' The answer was, yes. Colour prejudice in British society was exposed in a successful commercial film. And if critics were damning about the idea of exploring this area in a whodunnit, the retort was 'Why not?' If one could not have an enlightened essay on social morality in this country, a British film ready to face up to the problem of the position of black people in contemporary society, then a whodunnit like *Sapphire* is as good as any on which to hang a 'colour-bar problem' picture. Although it was worthwhile, it was doubtful whether *Flame in the Streets* might have helped or comforted any real family facing a similar problem, but these were early days in Britain's developing 'social' cinema, and time would attempt to restore the balance.

The Boulting Brothers are best remembered for their many comedies (*Happy is the Bride*; *I'm Alright Jack*; *Carlton Browne of the FO*; *Private's Progress*; *There's a Girl in My Soup*), but prior to these, some of their films reflected social aspects in more serious treatments. One such is *Fame is the Spur* (1947), which charts the rise and fall of a Labour politician. It's a study of idealism that ends in a peerage and isolation. Hamer Radshaw (Michael Redgrave) grows up in a North

Country mill town. His grandfather, a committed socialist, talks to Hamer of the people's battle for bread and liberty at Peterloo. Hamer marries Anne Artingstall, a young woman who shares his political views. He is elected labour MP for Saint Swithin's, and brandishes as his trademark a sword that dates back to Peterloo. He takes the sword to South Wales and incites striking miners to the point of riot. The military arrive and a miner is killed. Hamer will never quite recover from this, but his wife becomes more militant and joins the Suffragettes. She is imprisoned, and shortly after her release dies of consumption. Following a loss of public confidence, Hamer hangs on to his seat in the Labour victory and is made Lord Radshaw of Handforth. But the cost of his idealism has been too great.

In the year of its release, Labour Cabinet Ministers went to the pictures. Mr Attlee, the Prime Minister, went: so did his Deputy, Mr Bevin, and Sir Stafford Cripps, and a number of others. They went to see this film which was based on the rise, career and sad fall of Ramsay MacDonald. All politicians were determined that the future for Britain must be based on the principle of national unity. The Labour Movement of 1947 was proudly class-conscious. National unity was the cry, and *Fame is the Spur* was a film that gave a timely reminder for the Labour Movement of the period.

The film stays in the memory because of the touching performances of Michael Redgrave and Rosamund John (as Anne). Their scenes together effectively portray love and ideals balanced hand-in-hand; then, as ambition and circumstance ebb and flow, so the balance erodes and disillusionment sets in. The death of the miner, and Anne's own death, chillingly demonstrate how a blind faith in one's beliefs can also lead to a greater tragedy that affects the lives of millions.

This theme would be approached again, but in a more cynical fashion, at the start of a later decade. *No Love for Johnnie* (1960) has Peter Finch as the Labour MP also married to a woman of radical-left convictions. The new election sees Johnnie Byrne (Finch) back in the Cabinet at Westminster, but not in the post he was hoping for. His wife Alice (Rosalie Crutchley) leaves him because he is not as committed as she. Johnnie is hurt, but prefers to mourn the loss of the Cabinet post. Angry with his own Government, he is easily recruited by a pseudo-communist group, in order to make himself a nuisance. Increasingly disillusioned, he enters into various affairs, but nothing improves his state of mind. But then he is offered a better post in the Government – and at the same time his wife tries to revive their marriage. Then Johnnie discovers he might have got the previous job, but for his wife's political views.

The beauty of film is that changing times, social attitudes, historical events, can all be documented, albeit through the 'factional' eye of drama. The manners and morals of a century can be evaluated and re-appraised. Although there is no qustion but that time inevitably lessens the impact that sensitive issues have on the day, there is also no doubt that the films discussed in this chapter constantly remind us of the power and beauty of British films at their very best.

9

Things that Go Bump in the Night

Everyone loves to be frightened. That feeling of hushed expectancy in a crowded cinema, punctuated by the odd nervous giggle; the atmosphere is dark and tense, then suddenly broken by the awaited act of horror that jolts and shocks even though you knew it was coming. And then the relief, the mass exhalation, followed by the chatter and the laughter; and then the quiet, as the fear builds again. Right from the earliest days of silent movies, the film industry recognized the potential in scaring its filmgoers.

above, Felix Alymer in *A Place of One's Own*, 1944

Claude Rains in *The Clairvoyant*, 1934

below, Margaret Lockwood and Felix Alymer in *A Place of One's Own*, 1944

above right, Claude Rains in *The Clairvoyant*, 1934

right, Margaret Lockwood in *A Place of One's Own*, 1944

The Germans began it with *The Cabinet of Dr Caligari* (1919), a film that astounded audiences the world over, with its acutely disorientating sets and painted backdrops that made real the mad workings of a schizophrenic personality; and *Nosferatu* (1922), the story of a pale, deathly being who ghosts through life drawing sustenance only from the blood of others.

Hollywood climbed on to the bandwagon with the coming of the talkies. Bela Lugosi's unforgettable *Dracula* (1930), and the heartrending performance of Boris Karloff as the monster in *Frankenstein* (1931) spawned a cycle of sequels and re-makes that continue even in today's more cynical and sophisticated cinema. A costly version of *The Bride* released in 1985 to massive indifference from audiences and critics alike, demonstrated that the fifty years that have passed since James Whale's *Bride of Frankenstein* (1935) have bred a contempt based on too much familiarity. But the demand to be horrified, however, remains as intense as ever.

The British film industry entered the horror world in the 1930s as well – though, characteristically, in a much more subdued fashion. Unable to reproduce the fantastic sets and Gothic tone of Hollywood, the British horror film in the 1930s depended on a classic sense of introspection. The monsters didn't seem to be real, they seemed to be all in the mind.

Foretelling the future and predicting calamitous circumstances was the premise of one of Gainsborough's earliest efforts, *The Clairvoyant* (1934), wherein Claude Rains, a fraudulent psychic, earns a living from a rigged stage act. Inadvertently, and to his own growing horror and amazement, he discovers he really can predict the future. And what he sees isn't good. It's an underground disaster affecting the lives of many mineworkers. The problem is, how can he convince them it's really going to happen? *The Clairvoyant*, dealing as it does with the invasion of a mind by 'supernatural' events, is the first in a succession of British movies where one person is blessed or cursed with the problems of 'second sight.'

The next decade brought *A Place of One's Own* (1945), which took for its plotline a middle-aged couple moving to an elegant new home in the country. Disregarding reports that the old house is haunted, they settle in with their companion, a charming young woman called Annette (Margaret Lockwood), but as soon as they are settled, Annette becomes susceptible to the spirit of another young woman who died in the house some years previously. This frightening theme is further developed in a classic British film, made sixteen years later. Based on Henry James' fine novel *The Turn of the Screw*, *The Innocents* (1961) is a superb example of this genre of film-making. A governess (Deborah Kerr), is appointed to a country house to look after two young children, Miles and Flora. But she is not long in the job before she senses that the children are under 'supernatural' control of the previous governess and the gardener, who both died in a mysterious 'accident' which the children may have instigated. What may have befallen the dead couple is explored in the film's own sequel (or more accurately, 'prequel'), *The Nightcomers* (1972), which was directed by Michael Winner.

Although a pale reflection of its predecessor, *The Nightcomers* does boast a powerful performance from Marlon Brando as the evil gardener, Quint. The way he draws the prim young Miss Jessel (Stephanie Beacham; now Sable in the television Soap *The Colbys*) under the unhealthy influence is mesmerizing. One of the film's most haunting scenes occurs when Miles and Flora (the children), spy at night through Miss Jessel's bedroom window and witness her being roughly secured by rope to the bedposts. Equally, it is an explicit sex scene that lies at the heart of Britain's best psychic thriller, *Don't Look Now* (1973). Directed by Nicolas Roeg, who is perhaps the most enigmatic of British film-makers, it is a stunning labyrinth of themes, reflections, neuroses and supernatural fears.

John and Laura, a married couple in their thirties, live a comfortable life in the country, only to be thrown cruelly into psychological disarray by the accidental drowning of their daughter. But what worries John (Donald Sutherland) more than anything, is the fact that he was 'touched' with a premonition.

Christopher Lee in *Nothing But the Night*, 1972

Don't Look Now is as polished and complex a horror film as one could wish for, a glittering example of the very best of British. Daphne Du Maurier's short story was turned by the dazzling touch of Nicholas Roeg into a cautionary tale for the dissolute 1970s, rapidly collapsing after the false optimism of the Swinging Sixties. Another of Miss Du Maurier's stories had been filmed as long before as 1940 – *Rebecca*, originally published in 1938. This was a full-scale Hollywood production, albeit with an English director, the master of horror himself, Alfred Hitchcock. *Rebecca* is worth mentioning, though, because of its thematic similarities to other films discussed on these pages. It concerns a young woman who meets, falls in love with, and marries a man whilst she is travelling abroad as a companion for an old lady. She returns with the man, Mr De Winter (Laurence Olivier), to his large country estate, only to discover that he's been married before and the house seems to be cloyingly alive with the vengeful presence of the dead ex-wife, who, it transpires, committed suicide in such a way as to frame her husband for murder. Hitchcock, who could legitimately lay claim to being the greatest purveyor of 'shocks' in the business, sadly left England in 1939 and made most of his films thereafter in America (see chapter 5).

Of course not all horror films about vengeful dead ex-wives were necessarily horrifying – unless that is, you were the husband! *Blithe Spirit* (1945), the second full collaboration between the words of Noel Coward and the direction of David Lean (the first being *This Happy Breed* in 1944), was a comedy on that very subject. Little was actually done to Coward's original play, except that there was the occasional breaking-up of dialogue and the addition of a fresh line or two so as to move away from the living room (where the play had been set completely) and make the piece more cinematic. Coward himself wrote these changes in five days just before flying off to entertain troops in North Africa, and did them apparently on the back of an envelope. In an interview he explained: 'I just sat down with David [Lean] and asked – "Now what do you boys want? Sitting room to bedroom? Good. Got a pencil and a bit of paper? Here you are."'

Charles Condomine (Rex Harrison), a novelist, invites a medium to his home in Kent for a pleasant little seance. Unfortunately the medium, Madame Arcati (Margaret Rutherford), invokes the spirit of Condomine's first wife Elvira (Kay Hammond), who, much to the chagrin of the second wife Ruth (Constance Cummings), stays around to make everyone's life a misery. With the help of Madame Arcati, Ruth manages to send her back to the 'other side', but in a rage Elvira arranges for a car crash to kill Condomine. Instead, the crash kills Ruth – now there are two ghost wives bickering and squabbling over the hapless Condomine. Finally, in exasperation, he leaves the house, only to fall victim to another 'arranged' crash. He joins his wives on the 'other side'.

The production itself did not proceed so smoothly. Rank had decided to make another of its Technicolor specials (at the time only a few films in England could afford the expensive and rare film stock that was needed) and this produced problems in how to

represent the ghosts. They were solved by a complex lighting system. David Lean himself explained in a magazine interview: 'Kay Hammond's clothes were all grey, and the ghostly effect is got by following her around with a couple of green lights. Because we have to keep them fixed firmly on Kay though, and yet avoid the rest of the cast, we had to build the sets twice the normal size so as to have enough room to work in ... technically, the movie was murder.'

Emotionally too, there were difficulties. The atmosphere during shooting was tense, tempers were frayed between the actors, and Rex Harrison in particular felt uneasy in his part. Thankfully, however, Lean marshals his players superbly, and Margaret Rutherford as the batty Madame Arcati managed to draw out one of the most memorable performances of her career.

Blithe Spirit truly deserves its place in the horror genre, as Michael Anderegg observes in his excellent analysis of David Lean films: ' ... as frothy and inconsequential as *Blithe Spirit* may be on the surface, we can sense, not very far beneath the brittle dialogue and lovely drawing rooms and smart clothes, a dark and rather unpleasant world.'

An interesting aside to this film is that when the BBC wanted to show it on television in 1974, the original prints had shrunk so badly that they were unacceptable for presentation. So a painstaking job had to be done of putting together a brand new print frame by frame. It is sad to think that so many old British films still deteriorate in this manner.

Ghosts can be invoked by accident or by design, and a comical example of the former is *Don't Take it to Heart* (1944). Billed as an 'extravaganza', it features Richard Greene as Peter Hayward, a young man who visits Chaunduyt Court, an ancestral home. While there he is attracted by a photo of Mary, daughter of Lord Chaunduyt – and he stays on in the hope of meeting her by pretending to be interested in some old manuscripts unearthed by a bomb. The bomb has wrecked a Chaunduyt tomb and set free a

Richard Bird with Esma Cannon as the maid in *Don't Take it to Heart*, 1944

Richard Bird as the 'Terror of Chanduyt' in *Don't Take it to Heart*, 1944

Richard Bird in *Don't Take it to Heart*, 1944

wild prankster of a ghost. Involving himself in village politics, Peter proves (with the aid of the ghost) that nothing is as it seems.

Don't Take It to Heart was produced by Sydney Box a year before the great success of *The Seventh Veil*, for which he and his wife Muriel won the Oscar for Best Screenplay. They went on to become known for a series of realistic melodramas. Unfortunately, *Don't Take It to Heart* was not a popular film of its day: indeed its eccentric lunacy is far better suited to modern tastes. The American director Jeffery Dell, though, was not to realize this, and his film career was virtually over, when the film failed. Dell's novel, a satire on the British film industry, was aptly entitled *Nobody Ordered Wolves*.

Another film that had troubles on its release was *Black Narcissus* (1947), a torrid, atmospheric thriller of sexual repression amongst nuns in the heart of India. In America this proved far too sensitive and controversial a subject-matter for the censors. The late 1940s was a time when the power of the Catholic League of Decency was at its peak, and *Black Narcissus* was savaged: all the flashbacks of the nuns were cut (because they suggested that nuns might recall the past wistfully), as were the scenes of the nuns putting on silk stockings and lipstick, and one cut even changed the meaning of the story – suggesting that the 'evil' nun is driven mad because she is seduced, rather than because she wants to be.

However, the film still managed to scoop two Oscars, the Best Photography and Best Production Design. A curious nightmarish quality is built up throughout. Deborah Kerr plays Sister Clodagh, the Mother Superior, who is faced with the task of keeping the convent operating. Intimations of horror develop as the environment (heart, isolation and so on) plays tricks on the imagination, and eventually drives one nun, Sister Ruth (Kathleen Byron) to the very edge of madness and murder. Throughout the film the use of sound is unsettling: drums pick up the rhythm of heartbeats and rainstorms, and horns are carefully mixed in with the sound of the wind.

Another film which carefully manipulates the audience through technical skill is *A Place of One's Own* (1945). The makers of this slight but eerie ghost story were by coincidence all former newspapermen – producer R.J. Minney was the editor of the *Sunday Referee* and *Everybody's Weekly*; writer Brock Williams was a journalist in the West Country; and director Bernard Knowles had begun as a photographer on the *Detroit News*. These men were making their cinema débuts, and it is their background that gives the film such a feeling of realism. Knowles had previously worked as cameraman on *The 39 Steps* (1935) and *King Solomon's Mines* (1937); as director he decided that no special photographic trick effects would be used. Thus Ernst Thesiger (who plays the ghost) is presented for real, but with a soft accent and uttering mysterious words so as to suggest something unusual. Thesiger himself said, 'I looked at a distant object without focus and put a faraway tone in the voice – these are the secrets of being a ghost'.

Exteriors for the film were shot at Esher in Surrey at an old house which was reputed to have its own ghost, a white lady who walked the grounds on certain moonlit nights. During production there were no problems from her, though – instead there were flying bombs which dropped on the house and destroyed the front doors. Thankfully the prop people at the studio were able to build replicas at their workshops within a few hours.

It is the rich detail of the sets of *A Place of One's Own* that are so impressive. To devise them, the designer John Elphick worked with Thex Whistler, one of the most famous artists in Britain at the time, whose speciality was the Victorian era. Sadly, *A Place of One's Own* was his last screen work – he was killed in action in Normandy in July 1944.

Thirty years on from *The Clairvoyant*, its young writer-director Bryan Forbes covered similar territory in *Séance on a Wet Afternoon* (1964). Forbes, who had been an actor, turned screenwriter with *The League of Gentlemen*, an exciting thriller about disgruntled ex-Army officers banding together to rob a bank (see chapter 1). In 1962 he wrote and directed *Whistle Down the Wind*, a touching story of a young girl (Hayley Mills) finding an escaped convict in her father's barn, and believing he is Jesus returned to earth.

Kim Stanley in *Séance on a Wet Afternoon*, 1964

Séance on a Wet Afternoon is a thriller with elements of the 'other world'. Myra Savage (Kim Stanley) and her husband Billy (Richard Attenborough) are an odd couple. She is a professional medium, but unhappy at her lack of recognition. Forced by her mother to exercise her 'visionary' abilities, Myra has gone a little crazy. A plot is hatched to kidnap a child (most of Myra's séances are through her stillborn son Arthur), so that after the kidnap she will be able to 'show' the police the child's whereabouts. Because he loves her, Billy abducts a little girl, and they hide her in their own home. (The child believes she has had an accident and is in hospital.) Myra contacts the child's parents and tells them she can help, and the distraught mother (Nanette Newman) will clutch at anything. Everything seems to be going to plan, until the police call and Myra holds a séance; in her trance, she blurts out the truth.

Séance is a clever film, hinting at the delicate balance of grief and insanity. Its tension builds from a subtle, under-played style, but it ranks as one of the last of its type. British horror films had always implied rather than explicitly shown carnage and fear. Times, however, were changing.

After the record 1,635 million admissions to cinemas in Britain in 1946, they had slumped drastically by 1959 to 600 million. Many other forms of entertainment, including of course television, had contributed to the fall-off. In the 1950s the cinema devised new forms, new spectacles, to keep the public interested. Cinemascope, huge epics with casts of thousands, even 3-D was tried, but nothing really caught on in Britain. We were not conditioned to spending a night out at the cinema each week like the Americans, and attendances continued to drop. One thing that a new commercially minded film production company could try, though, was to give the audience that still remained something it couldn't get on television. And that was horror! Chills and thrills and all in colour to boot.

Hammer Films was formed in 1947 (or rather re-formed, because the company existed in the 1930s but under a different management). The owners were James Carreras and his son, and their plan was to make low-budget, almost B-feature movies that would titillate the punters. No film was to cost more than £20,000, and by this reckoning they calculated that five films a year would bring in £25,000-worth of profits from Britain alone. As the production budgets were so low, obviously they could not attract big-name stars. So they decided to choose catchy titles instead!

Hammer would operate almost like a mini-studio, developing a repertory company of directors and actors, so that each film would have a consistent look and style. A formula was born – Hammer would have an instant identification with its audience. When you saw the Hammer Films logo, you knew immediately what to expect! In the early 1950s Hammer cut its teeth on thrillers and sci-fi films such as *The Last Page* (1952) directed by Terence Fisher, a Hammer regular; *Four Sided Triangle* (1953); and *Spaceways* (1953), but soon horror was the watchword. *The Quatermass Experiment* (1955), directed by Val Guest, was the beginning; but if British audiences found that a shock, nothing prepared them for *Dracula* (1958). It was an incredible exercise in blood-letting, that had them queuing round the block.

Dracula was in colour, and furthermore the evil Count was played not by a monster, but by the tall, handsome Christopher Lee. When he advanced from the shadows to sink his teeth into the pale neck of an 'English Rose', audiences and the girl closed their eyes in near-ecstasy, the sensual undertones of Dracula suddenly became very clear overtones. Being bitten by a vampire was *sexy*!

Lurid advertising and the film's 'X' certificate caused an uproar of criticism and controversy. But Rank, releasing the film, was unconcerned, and the public packed the cinemas. *Dracula* was a hit.

James Carreras was also unconcerned, despite his being dubbed the 'King of Nausea'. His success was well worked out, as he explained: 'We've found a formula for spine-chillers that never misses ... You make the villain of your story look just like the good looking man, or the pretty girl, you might see on the underground any evening. You imagine you could trust him anywhere. Then suddenly you're alone with him – Wham! he starts to do terrible, awful, ghostly things!'

Dracula was directed by Terence Fisher with great flair, and Universal backed Hammer to film a re-make of *Frankenstein* (*The Curse of Frankenstein*, 1957). Universal now made available their whole

The classic opening scene from *Twins of Evil*, 1971

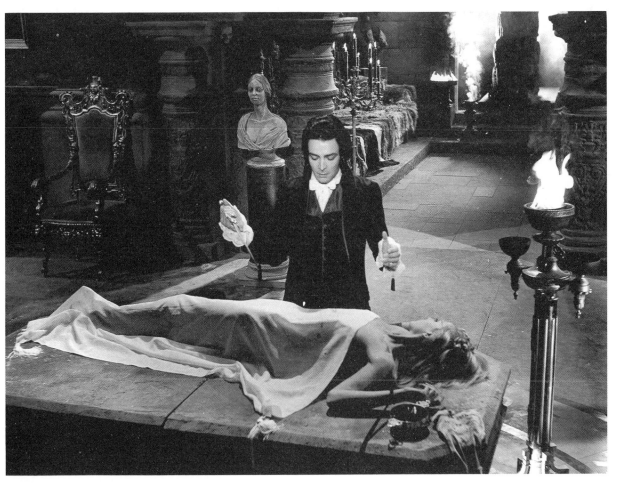

library of 1930s horror films to Hammer for re-makes. It was probably a shock to everyone at Hammer that these early films were such a success, but they paved the way for literally hundreds of films, utilizing every horror variation.

The Hammer *Dracula*, even viewed today, has the power to chill one's blood. Christopher Lee, and Peter Cushing as Van Helsing, the intrepid vampire-hunter, formed an uneasy blood pact to thrill audiences for the next twenty years. The 1960s cemented Hammer's reputation ... the prolific new workings of old themes continued unabated. *The Mummy* (1959), *The Curse of the Werewolf*, (1960) *The Phantom of the Opera* (1962), *Prince of Darkness* (1965), *The Plague of the Zombies* (1966) and *Rasputin, the Mad Monk* (1967) all got the Hammer treatment. *Rasputin* had Christopher Lee once more arousing women's fantasies; this time as the great seducer of the Russian Court.

Frankenstein and Dracula survived into the 1970s, but by 1973 both had dwindled in popularity. Interestingly, the relaxation of censorship at the end of the 1960s produced a brief cycle of more 'adult' Hammer films: *The Vampire Lovers* (1970), *Lust for a Vampire* (1970) and *Twins of Evil* (1971). These capitalized on pretty young starlets prepared to bare their all in the name of Hammer. The sexual aspects of vampirism are taken to greater heights as women sink their fangs into various parts of not-too-unwilling young men. In fact, *Twins of Evil* is something of a Gothic masterpiece.

Based on characters created by J. Sheridan Le Fanu (mainly the lesbian vampire, Carmilla), and directed by John Hough from a screenplay by Tudor Gates (who also scripted *Vampire Lovers* and *Lust for a Vampire*) it combines Puritan zeal with the decadent lusts of vampirism. Maria and Frieda are twins, who move from Vienna to a little village called Karnstein, to live with their Uncle Gustav Weil (Peter Cushing), who is the head of an obsessive Puritan sect. A neighbour, Lord Karnstein, inadvertently reincarnating his ancestor Mircalla, becomes a vampire. Frieda, on visiting Lord Karnstein's castle, is seduced and vampirized. She in turn bites others, both male and female, until her sister Maria and her fiance Anton, with the help of the crazed Weil, attack Kernstein and burn the castle.

The twins of the title were actually played by real twins, Madeleine and Mary Collinson, whose likeness was so great that on set it was apparently impossible for the crew to tell the two actresses apart. On screen, however, the gimmick doesn't really come off, and it is left for director John Hough to create the horror with the mists of the Pinewood Studio sets. His aims were simple: 'If cinemagoers don't scream and shudder, I feel I shall have failed.'

For the critics, he did succeed. Nigel Andrews, writing in *Monthly Film Bulletin*, stated that "the reincarnation of Countess Mircalla, an ectoplasmic shape rising from the sarcophagus and floating in hooded silence towards the terrified Karnstein, is a tour de force. And though *Twins of Evil* has its share of the usual Hammer deficiencies – insipid juveniles and some over-familiar Pinewood locations – it is easily the best of their Vampire films for some time."

Mircalla could be a direct relative of Countess Elizabeth Nadasdy, played by Ingrid Pitt in *Countess Dracula* (1970). The character is based

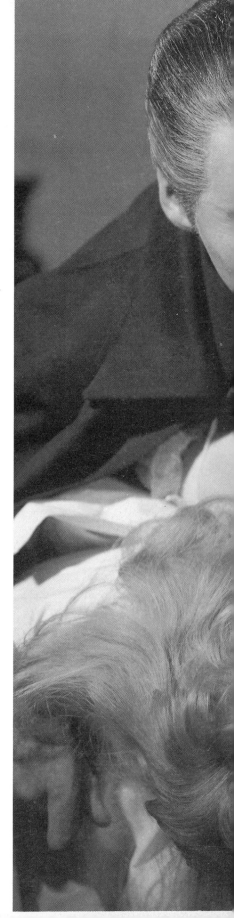

right, Christopher Lee in *Dracula*, 1958

on the real-life Hungarian, Countess Bathory, who in the seventeenth century, bathed in virgins' blood to rejuvenate her flesh and retain her youth. Directed by Peter Sasdy (hopefully no relation to Nadasdy!), it was quite a compelling addition to Hammer's library. It was the first production that Hammer made in association with Rank.

Elizabeth Nadasdy discovers that virgins' blood does wonders for the skin. After killing a chambermaid, Elizabeth poses as her own daughter in order to seduce a young hussar, Imre Toth (Sandor Eles). The ploy succeeds, but Elizabeth needs a constant supply of blood to remain young. With the help of her faithful Captain Dobi (Nigel Green), she abducts and kills many young women from neighbouring villages. During her wedding to Imre, she suddenly becomes an old hag. She accidentally kills Imre in her hunger for fresh blood. She is locked in a cell and awaits the hangman. The women in the village whisper her name, and pronounce her 'Countess Dracula'.

Countess Dracula was the first film to latch on to the thought that vampire legend was started by women. The story of Countess Bathory actually began when by accident she hit a chambermaid so hard that blood from the girl's nose spurted into her face. When she washed the blood off and looked in the mirror, she found her skin appeared more beautiful and much whiter. So began her life of murder. At Countess Bathory's trial in 1611, it was found she had killed more than a hundred virgins (although only eighty were found), who had all been tortured before slowly being drained of blood.

Another historical villain to whom the folks at Hammer were attracted was Jack the Ripper. His best incarnation under Carreras and Co. was in *Hands of the Ripper* (1971). Here the 'supernatural' is used through a fake medium. Anna, Jack the Ripper's daughter, is acting as a 'voice' during the séances. She has become psychologically disturbed as a result of the actions of her father, and murders seem to follow in her footsteps. Psychiatrist Dr John Pritchard (Eric Porter) deduces that Anna may be the killer. His Freudian methods corroborate this, and when he pursues her to St Paul's Cathedral, he catches her in the act of murder. Under a hypnotic trance she falls from the Whispering Gallery to her death.

The curious idea of Jack the Ripper's daughter carrying on the tradition, albeit subconsciously, is effective. The scenes of the medium's discovery of Jack's identity, coupled with the daughter's homicidal tendencies, are indeed frightening. The film was again directed by the talented Peter Sasdy, who was born in Hungary, but emigrated at an early age to England. He was highly rated for his prestigious BBC productions (such as *Wuthering Heights* and *Spoils of Poynton*), before he went under contract at Hammer. *Hands of the Ripper*, despite its going to excess, is a full expression of his skills, especially in his handling of the performance of Anghared Rees, who was making her film debut at the age of twenty-three. The final confrontation between Pritchard and Anna in St Paul's has a wonderfully unworldly feeling to it. Pritchard arrives just in time to prevent Anna from murdering his own daughter Laura (Jane

Ingrid Pitt and Nigel Green in *Countess Dracula*, 1970

right, Ingrid Pitt in *Countess Dracula*, 1970

far right, Eric Porter and Angharad Rees in *Hand of the Ripper*, 1971

Merrow). From the nave, Pritchard gazes up into the Whispering Gallery where the murder attempt is happening, and implores Anna to join him. With a beatific smile, Anna complies. She releases Laura, perches on the handrail, then steps over and off. Her cape billows, and she seems to take forever to reach the ground. When she does, she makes contact softly; her death is like landing on a pillow of clouds.

That memorable cinematic flourish virtually signified the end of Hammer's reign as the ultimate purveyors of Grand Guignol and Gothic grossness. The early 1970s produced only one more film of merit, *Frasnkenstein and the Monster from Hell* (1973). The others were mainly sub-standard, or just plain disastrous, and besides, Hammer couldn't hope to compete with the very realistic group of films that were heralding a new era in film-making at the start of the 1970s. An unpleasant era, some critics would say, but then again, that's what they said on *Dracula's* release back in 1958.

Times were changing. The early 1970s were marked by two devastating British films, Sam Peckinpah's *Straw Dogs* (1971) and Ken Russell's *The Devils* (1971). In the former, the notion of a man and his wife (Dustin Hoffman and Susan George) trapped in their house while a gang of psychopathic yokels rail around outside was used as a truly horrible fable, made vividly real by the increase in Britain's crimes of violence. In *The Devils*, the world Russell creates is so corrupt and insane, so hysterical, disease-ridden and violent as to almost defy the imagination. These films were going beyond the ancient stories which Hammer tried to revive, and presenting warped reflections of our own society. Hammer's days were definitely numbered.

The new horror films were based on the psychological terrors of twentieth-century life. In this realm, Rank's last film as a production company was a worthy arrival. *Bad Timing* (1980) is about a relationship that goes sour. And wry observers of the British film industry noted at the time that the film's name was somehow appropriate to Rank's sad withdrawal from active film-making. *Bad Timing*, directed by Britain's most sylish director, Nicholas Roeg, really wasn't for the squeamish. There is an oppressive, doomed relationship between Alex (Art Garfunkel), an American psychiatrist working in Vienna, and Milena (Theresa Russell), a wilful young American woman drifting round the bars and clubs of middle Europe. Alex is spotted by Milena, and wishes to possess him completely. Through a series of intricate flashbacks, we watch the two meet, fall in love and grow apart. But there's nothing ordinary about it. Milena has taken an overdose and is having her stomach pumped in the hospital. A dour police officer, Netusil (Harvey Keitel), is questioning Alex, because there is something odd in the timing. Something strange and disquieting. The film quickly becomes a nightmare vision of Alex's subconscious.

Bad Timing is an engrossing, compulsive, disorientating movie, as it seeks to re-evaluate relationships and our responses to them. Nicholas Roeg's mastery of his medium is wholly absorbing; we are sucked deeper into Alex's besotted fantasies. It is a truly disturbing film, and as dark a nightmare as one is likely to find anywhere. He commented: 'I wanted to reach down inside people to permeate their emotions ... It was chosen as the final film at the close of the Berlin Film Festival ... what a way to finish. Not a very happy ending.' Indeed, the film quickly became one of the most controversial of the year, only gaining an 'X' certificate when a certain scene was cut. It divided audiences and critics alike, but its mixture of crude visual and artistic thought is certainly a perfect reflection of the modern horror.

left and below, Art Garfunkel in *Bad Timing*, 1980

The Eccentrics

'The eccentricities of genius, Sam,' said Mr Pickwick.

Mr Pickwick, Dickens's great comic creation, was referring to that elusive quality which he himself undoubtedly possessed, and which is common to all genuine eccentrics – there is about them all an air of genius. Theatre and literature are crowded with these 'special' people. Long after the heroes, heroines and villains have faded from our thoughts, the eccentrics are still there, firmly implanted in our memory. Shakespeare's Falstaff, Wilde's Lady Bracknell, Wodehouse's Bertie Wooster – these are but a few of the characters who have become part of the national heritage. They are some of the legends of literature, but it is clear that their characteristics are so well defined, so well drawn, that they must have surely all been based very closely on real eccentrics. However brilliant the author may be, however powerful the imagination, the creation of classic eccentrics owes more to the skill of observation than to any other attribute. In the world of cinema, there have been equally memorable eccentrics; character actors and actresses who extend their performances way beyond the scope of their roles, adding an extra indefinable dimension to all that they do and say. And the British cinema has been rich indeed in such people.

Sam and Mr Pickwick from *Pickwick Papers*, by Charles Dickens

These are not those actors who are able to put on the make-up and the mantle to portray a role, however convincing they may be. The cinema eccentrics are a breed apart. They do play their parts – often brilliantly – but always that essential ingredient, an intangible, unique quality that marks them out as 'different' comes shining through, transcending the script, the camera work or even the most inspired director.

A.E. Mathews, known affectionately as 'Matty' to everyone in the entertainment industry, was born in 1869. It is difficult to believe that when he began his career in films in the early 1920s, he played romantic leads, for his later performances have come to represent the archetypal English eccentric. And he was the real thing – stories of his off-set eccentricities abound.

But many of the tales spread about him were started by himself. For example, he was supposed to be very carefree about learning his lines for a play, and used to give the impression that he was constantly on the brink of 'drying up' – yet it is known that he devoted long hours to studying a part, and his relaxed, almost absent-minded, approach to his work was merely a well-calculated pose. It did sometimes backfire on him, and on one occasion when he met George Bernard Shaw, a playwright whom he much admired, he told Shaw that he had never been in one of his plays. 'Nor will you be,' Shaw replied acidly, 'I prefer actors to speak the lines I write. I hear that you prefer your own.' This remark only momentarily ruffled Mathews, who could probably lay claim to being the oldest working actor of them all.

He made his stage début at the Prince's Theatre in 1887 in a play called *Held by the Enemy*, in which he played every part but one. Yet to Alfred Edward Mathews (he rarely used his full christian names), this would have been par for the course. It was part of his stage upbringing to turn his hand to anything and everything theatrical. He was the son of a Christie minstrel, and must have watched his father as he was singing, dancing and playing a variety of musical instruments, engaging in 'repartee'—as joke-telling was referred to in those days—and then being a part-time stage manager and set designer. A minstrel had to do the lot, and his son was left in no doubt that he should be able to do the same. His experiences in a long and busy career often read like a catalogue of catastrophes. He was laughed and booed off the stage in Australia. In South Africa the audience was so critical of his efforts that they fired revolvers at the ceiling. And in New York, during the first of his many Broadway seasons, he was doped and robbed in Chinatown, and sent back to England on a boat, steerage class.

But 'Matty' the Unpredictable was also unflappable. He could laugh at all types of misfortune because he never took himself or life too seriously, and this was probably the secret of his success. He claimed to have earned over £1 million, a great deal of money in those days—and he blew it all! 'What I haven't thrown away, those damned Inland Revenue people have collared.' he once said.

A.E. Matthews and Cecil Parker in *The Chiltern Hundreds*, 1949

A.E. Matthews and Cecil Parker in *The Chiltern Hundreds*, 1949

At the age of eighty, A.E. Mathews made his film début as a 'star' in the screen version of William Douglas Home's comedy about impoverished aristocracy, *The Chiltern Hundreds* (1949). He was surrounded by a strong cast, including David Tomlinson, Marjorie Fielding and Cecil Parker. Mathews said of Parker, 'He acted me off the set.' But although Parker as the loyal butler was splendid, this was always Matty's film. He was the personification of all those dotty English peers who ignore the big issues and concentrate on trivia. With Mathews in *The Chiltern Hundreds*, it was his obsession with marauding rabbits invading his grounds that seemed to occupy all his waking hours. There seemed to be so much of Mathews himself in this role for, in truth, he was straight out of a Wodehousian world of absent-minded Earls and Squires in Bertie Wooster-land. He had made the Douglas Home character fit him like a well-tailored Norfolk Jacket, having been involved with the original stage play from the outset.

On the first night of the stage play *The Chiltern Hundreds* in 1949, after his first exit the audience rose to give him a tumultuous ovation. A fellow actor who was standing in the wings turned to him and said, 'Congratulations old boy, I've never heard such applause on a first act exit.' Quick as a blast from a double-barrelled shotgun, Mathews replied, 'Well, you know what that means – they don't think I'll live till Act II.' He was at the time seventy-seven.

A.E. Mathews died peacefully in his bed at the age of ninety on 26 July 1960. 'It was' said Robert Morley – by no means a lightweight in the eccentricity stakes himself – 'the most unlikely thing he ever did.'

It would be difficult to imagine that there was ever a more lovable lady eccentric in fiction or in fact than Margaret Rutherford. She must surely reign supreme as queen of all those dotty upper-middle-class women who at once combine impeccable manners with an utterly chaotic lifestyle. She was, in truth, a genuine eccentric.

Margaret Rutherford was born in Balham on 11 May, 1892. The original family name was Benn, but her father decided to change it to Rutherford because he felt it was a more aesthetic name for a writer. The fact that Ernest Rutherford was not a writer but a traveller in silks in India at the time was, to him, immaterial. It does, however, provide a clue to the background of Margaret Rutherford, showing us that if eccentric people are not exactly born, they are shaped very early in life. She lived in India as an infant, and was left an orphan at a very young age. Then her mother's sister, Bessie, who lived in Wimbledon, became responsible for bringing little Margaret up. And it was here that the seeds of eccentricities which had been sown in Margaret by her father were given the opportunity to bloom, for 'Aunt Bessie' herself was completely unconventional too. Margaret was encouraged to live in a world of make-believe, as her aunt was totally besotted with the theatre, and often used to stage what were known as 'family theatricals'.

When Margaret, who used to suffer from back trouble, complained of pain, Aunt Bessie would take command and insist that she should lie quite motionless on the floor while Bessie read to her in French. If there were some kind of logic in believing that reading in French would ease the pain of back ache, then perhaps only a Rutherford would understand it. We lesser mortals would remain, as we were with so many of her film and theatre performances, utterly bemused but always fascinated.

Young Margaret Rutherford, having studied piano for many years, became a piano teacher, cycling all round Wimbledon to give her pupils their hour's worth of scales and arpeggios. She was, she admitted, not a good teacher, as she was rather tetchy and impatient. But if none of her pupils ever made the concert platform, Margaret at least became a first-class cyclist, and this skill was put to good effect later on when she played Madame Arcati in Noel Coward's *Blithe Spirit*. She used to come whizzing on to the stage and brake within inches of the footlights. It always got a round of applause. But that was far into the future, for Margaret started her theatrical career rather late in life, beginning at the age of thirty-three when she auditioned for the Old Vic School. Throughout her prepared piece her new shoes, bought especially for this auspicious occasion, constantly squeaked. Perhaps this amused the great Lilian Bayliss, the guiding light of the acting constellations which included Dame Edith Evans, Sir John Gielgud, Lord Olivier and Sir Ralph Richardson, for she took on the very green, but desperately enthusiastic, Rutherford.

After her distinguished career on the stage, Margaret Rutherford ventured into the film world, making her début in *Dusty Ermine* (1936). Thereafter, films became very much part of her life, and that warm, almost whimsical eccentricity that was so much her off-stage

Margaret Rutherford in *Blithe Spirit*, 1945

personality was being seen by a much wider audience. Indeed, her unique style was appreciated throughout the world, and especially in America.

In 1943 she was cast in an Anthony Asquith production called *The Demi Paradise*, whose title was changed for the US market to *Adventures for Two*. For once Margaret, playing the organizer of a village pageant and a general 'do-gooder', was nearly overshadowed by a village full of eccentrics – Felix Aylmer, Joyce Grenfell and many others, all bringing to their parts that dreamy, middle-class, absent-minded quality that is the very essence of British eccentricity. Laurence Olivier, who was playing the role of a visiting, and very bemused, Russian inventor in the film, told her, 'I've been in films for years now, and I'm just getting the knack of it." Margaret responded, 'My word, I've got a bit of work to do.'

The Demi Paradise contains a scene that takes place during an air raid, which must rate now as one of the funniest ever shot during those dark days of the War. Whilst a bridge game is played in a splendidly designed upper middle-class drawing room of the period, and genteel conversation is in progress, a lady cellist, armed with her bulky instrument, enters. She has arrived to play a musical accompaniment in the back garden of the house to the song of the nightingale, which is to be broadcast live on BBC radio. They ignore

Anthony Asquith directing *Demi Paradise*, 1943

146

Felix Alymer in *Demi Paradise*, 1943

the bombs, the enemy planes droning overhead, and the searchlights probing the skies. The only concession the little group make to this air raid is that the drawing-room lights are switched off, before the french windows are opened and the curtains parted to allow the lady to take her seat in the garden. With great dignity, the musician bows her way through the strains of a cello classic, whilst the nightingale, obliging little chap that he is, trills away for all he's worth, much to the delight of the occupants of the drawing room and, presumably, the radio listeners. Olivier, as the visiting Russian guest, surveys the whole scene with barely concealed amazement.

Generally speaking though, scene-stealing on stage or screen from Margaret Rutherford is rare indeed. She admits to having developed, over the years, the art of underacting, whilst making her eyes expressive, her nose twitch, and her chin tremble – not, of course, all at the same time. Her brilliance remains on film now for all to see and admire again and again, whether in major or minor roles. Her characters are unforgettable: Madame Arcati in *Blithe Spirit*; the maddening playwright to Robert Morley's director in *Curtain Up* (she always said that Morley understood her more than almost anyone, and was a great friend); the District Nurse in *Miranda*; the romantic governess, Miss Prism, playing opposite the formidable Edith Evans in *The Importance of Being Earnest*; and a cameo role where she broke all the rules, by scene-stealing from animals, as the pet-shop owner in *An Alligator Named Daisy*. In 1963 – again in a smallish role in *The VIPs*, she won her coveted Oscar for Best Supporting Actress, playing the part of the lovable Lady Brighton.

Margaret Rutherford would never have called herself a star, but the stars she worked with, a list of whom would read like the motion-picture industry's *Who's Who*, all felt the same way about

above left, Miles Mallison in *The Importance of Being Earnest*, 1952

above, Margaret Rutherford and Donald Sinden in *An Alligator Named Daisy*, 1956

Margaret Rutherford and Robert Morley in *Curtain Up*, 1952

Margaret Rutherford in *Miranda*, 1947

right, Michael Redgrave and Margaret Rutherford in *The Importance of Being Earnest*, 1952

below, Glynis Johns in *Miranda*, 1947

below right, Edith Evans in *The Importance of Being Earnest*, 1952

her. To all of them she was a 'superstar' – and they had one other thing in common – they loved her.

Scots eccentrics stand head and shoulders above the rest. Into this category comes a man who was touched by genius and had all those other endearing qualities that put him a class of his own as a top-ranking film eccentric. His name – Alastair Sim.

Sim was born in Edinburgh on 9 October, 1900, the son of an Edinburgh JP. He was educated at the James Gillespie School in his home city, and at the university there. He began earning a living by lecturing to Divinity students on elocution and phonetics at New College, Edinburgh, and although he never had any serious intention of becoming a professional actor, he formed a theatrical society with a few of his students, and produced poetry and drama at Oxford and Bath, as well as at Edinburgh University.

It was the famous playwright, John Drinkwater, who first spotted that Alastair Sim had a special talent for acting, and although Sim had never wished to do anything theatrical other than produce, Drinkwater insisted that he had what it took to become a fine actor, and gave him a list of his own very considerable theatre contracts. As a result, Sim's stage career began with a minor part in *Othello* at the Savoy Theatre in 1930, with Paul Robeson in the lead. Two years later he joined the Old Vic, where the producer Harcourt Williams saw his potential as a comedian. It took until 1935 for him to gain critical acclaim, and this he achieved by a splendid (and what is now regarded as a characteristic Sim) performance, as a sycophantic bank manager, in the West End comedy *Youth at the Helm*.

A year before his theatre success in 1934, he had made his first film, *Riverside Murder*. A few years later he was playing with the most eccentric bunch of comedians ever brought together as a team in Britain, those Royal favourites, the Crazy Gang. In the film *Alf's Button Afloat* (1938 – see chapter 4.), Sim played a 'genie' who would instantly appear to obey the commands of his master, Bud Flanagan, whenever he rubbed a button which had been melted down from the original Aladdin's Lamp. Sim not only held his own against these unpredictable comics, but in many cases completely out-acted them. He could be extremely extrovert in his work – and indeed that came across in such films as *Sailing Along* (1938), *Cottage to Let* (1941), *Waterloo Road* (1944), *Green for Danger* (1946), and *The Happiest Days of Your Life* (1949) – but he was, in reality, a most private man, rarely granting interviews to the press, and never allowing a biography to be written. He was mortified at the idea of writing his own life story.

Sim enjoyed his reclusive lifestyle, and was everyone's idea of a benign eccentric uncle. But he did have his moments of tetchiness, as for example when he was appearing in the West End in the play *The Magistrate*. One night a very handsome man and an attractive blonde lady came to call on him in his dressing room. The man, who spoke with a soft American accent, said: 'Sir, I've learned more in one night from watching your performance than I have in ten years of acting in theatre and films.' Sim was politely indifferent to

above, Alastair Sim and the Crazy Gang

below right, Alastair Sim in *Alf's Button Afloat*, 1938

top right, Alastair Sim and Jessie Matthews in *Sailing Along*, 1938

right, George Cole in *Cottage to Let*, 1941

151

the compliment, and summarily ushered the man and woman out. Sim's dresser, who witnessed the incident in stunned silence, turned to him after the couple had left, and said: 'Do you know who they were?' 'No,' replied Sim. 'Paul Newman and his wife, Joanne Woodward,' the ashen-faced dresser informed him. Sim still seemed unimpressed, clearly knowing very little of their Hollywood reputation. But he later watched some of Newman's films and was staggered by his talent. He was filled with regret about the casual manner he had adopted with Newman, and wrote a long letter of apology to him. Newman responded with typical generosity, and the two remained firm friends for many years.

Sim had a style of acting uniquely his own, and although his mannerisms were often copied by lesser performers, and his voice mimicked by others, this lugubrious, thoughtful and gentle eccentric stamped a seal of originality on his acting that will never be equalled.

If Alastair Sim could prove conclusively that eccentricity in entertainers is not an English prerogative by arranging to be born in Edinburgh, then Cicely Courtneidge could go much further in making the point – to the other side of the world, in fact. For this comedy actress, who was most certainly eccentric in the extreme, was born in Sydney, New South Wales, and she had a fair dinkum start to her eccentric lifestyle by arranging to be born on All Fools' Day 1893. Her father, Robert, a principal light comedian, was appearing in the show *Esmeralda* when Cicely made her début into the world. The landlady of the house in which they were lodging rushed excitedly into the theatre and shouted the news about the new baby at the top of her voice, right from the back of the stalls and right in the middle of his performance. The audience at once broke into spontaneous applause and cheers. At only a few minutes old, Cicely had already stopped the show. She was, in fact, christened Esmeralda after this spectacular incident. But she hated the name and plumped for her middle name – Cicely.

Cicely Courtneidge came to Britain in her teens, and after many disappointments at the outset of her career in music hall, went on to become a major star of the musical comedy theatre, and of British film musicals. But although she was a star in her own right, and one who had the energy of a megaton bomb, it is for her long-time professional partnership with her husband, Jack Hulbert, who almost qualified to be in the eccentric class himself, that she is best remembered. Together they starred in one smash-hit show after another, and in many a hit comedy film, such as *The Ghost Train* (1931), and *Jack's the Boy* (1932). Cicely also established herself as Miss Vitality with star solo performances in such British film musicals as *Soldiers of the King* (1933) and *Aunt Sally* (1934), and others which were perhaps less successful but, nevertheless, did manage to capture some of that idiosyncratic whirlwind essence that aroused so much admiration in her fellow artistes – performers of the standing of Lord Olivier, Sir John Mills, and Noel Coward, who simply 'adored her'. She was, without doubt, the best company in the world to be with – always bubbling with enthusiasm, and

above, Cecily Courtneidge in *Soldiers of the King*, 1933

below, Peter Sellers and Cyril Cusack in *Waltz of the Toreadors*, 1962

recounting stories of her offbeat lifestyle to gales of raucous laughter.

When Cicely Courtneidge was at last persuaded to write her life story, she realized that she did not have all the material she needed to set about the task, so instead of ploughing through her well-kept diaries and press-cuttting books, with typical illogicality she decided to write to the Editor of *The Times*:

> 15, South Audley Street,
> London W.1.
>
> To the Editor,
> The Times,
> Printing House Square,
> London, E.C.4.
>
> Dear Sir,
>   I am collecting material for a biography of Miss Cicely Courtneidge, the actress. I would be most grateful if anyone who has any letters or anecdotes, or other data about Miss Cicely Courtneidge, the actress, would send them to me at the address above.
>
>   I remain, Sir,
>   Your obedient servant,
>   Cicely Courtneidge.

The letter was solemnly read by the Editor and duly printed. It prompted an immediate response from her friends, but one in particular sent to her address by hand amused her enormously. It read:

> Dear Miss Courtneidge,
>   With reference to your letter in the 'Times' asking for details about the life of Miss Cicely Courtneidge, the actress. You ought to know all about her by now.
>   I remain, Madame,
>   Your obedient servant,
>   Jack Hulbert.
>
> 15, South Audley Street,
> London, W.1.

Ah! They don't make eccentrics like that any more, and the world is undoubtedly a sadder place without them.

John Stuart Mill put it like this: 'Eccentricity has always abounded when and where strength of character has abounded' – and no one would argue with that.

Acknowledgements

Our grateful thanks to everyone who helped us in the preparation of this book – especially Fred Turner, Keith Robertson, Chris Towle, Sandra Ford, Derek Long, Howell Thomas, Tony Stratton Smith, David Gideon Thomson, Roy Baird, Patrick Doyle, Cathy McKnight, and Holly Fogg. And, as always, very special thanks to G.I.S. Patricia Helen Lowry, Gomer and Elsie Morris, and last but by no means least, Doris and Alf Bartlett.

The authors and producers are grateful to Rank Film Distributers for permission to use their photographs.